Stewarding the Anointing

THE CODE OF CONDUCT FOR THE KINGDOM

PeriSean B. Hall

PeriSean Enterprises

CEDAR HILL, TX

Copyright © 2020 PeriSean Enterprises
445 East FM 1382, Suite 3-158
Cedar Hill, TX/75104

For more information, visit the author's website at www.perisean.com

Unless otherwise noted, all Scripture quotations are taken from the King James Version of the Bible. Scripture quotations marked ESV are taken from the Holy Bible, English Standard Version. Copyright © 2001 by Crossway Bibles, a division of Good News Publishers. Used by permission. Scripture quotations marked NASB are taken from the New American Standard Bible, copyright © 1960, 1962, 1963, 1968, 1971, 1972, 1973, 1975, 1977, 1995 by The Lockman Foundation. Used by permission. www.Lockman.org. Scripture quotations marked NKJV are taken from the New King James Version®. Copyright © 1982 by Thomas Nelson. Used by permission. All rights reserved. Scripture quotations marked NLT are from the Holy Bible, New Living Translation, copyright © 1996, 2004, 2007. Used by permission of Tyndale House Publishers, Inc., Wheaton, IL 60189. All rights reserved. Scripture quotations marked NIV are taken from the Holy Bible, New International Version®, NIV®. Copyright © 1973, 1978, 1984, 2011 by Biblica, Inc.® Used by permission of Zondervan. All rights reserved worldwide. www.zondervan.com. The "NIV" and "New International Version" are trademarks registered in the United States Patent and Trademark Office by Biblica, Inc.®

Library of Congress Cataloging-in-Publication Data: An application to register this book for cataloging has been submitted to the Library of Congress.

International Standard Book Number (ISBN): 978-0-578-62615-4

While the author has made every effort to provide accurate internet addresses at the time of publication, neither the publisher nor the author assumes any responsibility for errors or for changes that occur after publication.

Printed in the United States of America

Contents

Why We Need Order 1
Who Is the Church? 11
The Anointing 19
Management of the Anointing 29
Activating the Anointing 37
The Principle of Oneness 43
Protocol of Worship 47
A Warning About Witchcraft 55
Initiating Relationships 63
Protocol of Expectation 73
Protocol of Access 77
Protocol of God's Glory 83
Protocol of Divine Assignment 99
Why Does It Matter? 109
Bibliography 111
About the Author 115
Author's Resource Page 117

Foreword

IT IS WITH GREAT JOY that I encourage you to open your heart and learn from a pro. PeriSean knows her way around protocol. It takes a sixth sense to be able to discern the situations, know the right response, and understand who is in charge and how to respond to that person—to know those who are moving with authority and power and those who are just moving with power.

I have enjoyed PeriSean's counsel and friendship for several decades, and I knew the source of a lot of her wisdom, her beautiful mother. PeriSean not only knows the principles of protocol she writes about; she also lives them and is able to teach them to others.

There is an unspoken and unseen order behind the scenes. PeriSean awakens us to these spiritual and natural principles and laws that are hidden. She walks in both. You will enjoy the wisdom she has gained, and the excellence of insight in these pages will help you walk in your anointing with purpose and power and, now, with understanding and insight. There is nothing worse than being where you are supposed to be but not be ready to receive what God wants to give you. Get ready by reading and studying this book.

Current leaders are looking for the next generation. Most of the new leaders of this generation don't respect the protocol of the natural realm or even the spiritual realm. They are passed over because they lack the respect and understanding they need to move in these powerful circles.

Most of us hit our heads against these secrets for years without ever gaining true revelation. This dramatically hinders our growth and ability to move into what God has for us. PeriSean lays out the principles that will prepare you and me to walk in power. Be quiet, be still, rest, and listen. Let her guide you into truths that I haven't seen written anywhere else.

This book will bless you beyond measure. Open your heart, get a notebook to write down the insights in these pages, and apply these truths to your life. You will learn how to walk with the giants, humble yourself to reach the broken, and sing and dance with those who rejoice. PeriSean has done it all. May God open the eyes of the church to see and hear this writer-prophet as she declares natural and supernatural laws and principles that will change our lives.

—DR. ROD STODGHILL

Introduction

I HAVE HUMBLY ACCEPTED God's commission to write this book for the church of Jesus Christ. In this literary account, my primary focus is to assist the church in reexamining her responsibility to stewardship. I will also review godly principles of divine order, also referred to as protocol. All Christians have a responsibility to manage everything God has entrusted to our care, including how we nurture our relationship with Him, ourselves, and others, and how we manage our bodies and our time. Succinctly put, we are stewards, not owners, and stewardship is the area where God will hold us accountable.

What is stewardship? Nationally known preacher and pastor Tony Evans, ThD, says this: "The proper definition of stewardship is given by its author, God Himself. The Bible begins with God creating, talking, and doing. He made the earth and mankind, and therefore He is the owner of all things. God created and then gave responsibility to humanity to manage His creation. We don't own anything on earth; it's all God's property. The Bible is very clear about this. In Exodus 19:5, God says, 'All the earth is Mine.' In Psalm 89:11, the psalmist said to God, 'The world and all it contains, You have founded them.'"

While stewardship is "resource management" in a God-given assignment, I believe protocol is a God-instituted system, process, or blueprint by which we function in a God-given assignment. Protocols are in place so that divine order is established and maintained. First Chronicles 28:12 says God gave David the plans to the temple that his son Solomon was to build: "He gave him the plans of all that the Spirit had put in his mind for the courts of the temple of the Lord and all the surrounding rooms, for the treasuries of the temple of God and for the treasuries for the dedicated things" (NIV). God not only tells us what to do, He provides a blueprint to show us specifically how He wants things done. At the head of that blueprint is unwavering love—love for God, love for people, and love for the plans and purposes of God. Without God's exact blueprint, plans fail, and chaos and ruin will be the result.

The chaos in the world today is a direct result of the chaos in the church, which is due to the fact that we have not followed God's blueprint. The need in this day and time is order in the church, because judgment will surely begin in the house of the Lord, as 1 Peter 4:17 says: "For the time is come that judgment must begin at the house of God: and if it first begin at us, what shall the end be of them that obey not the gospel of God?" (KJV).

Believers have a mandate to fulfill the first and greatest commandment, which is to "love the Lord your God with all your heart and with all your soul and with all your mind" (Matt. 22:37, NIV). Before the church can wholeheartedly serve God, we must first develop the most important relationship ever known to mankind—our relationship with God. He has called us to love Him by worshipping Him in spirit and in truth (John 4:24). When we foster a thriving, intimate relationship with the Father through Jesus Christ, we will be better prepared to execute our God-given assignments and responsibilities with excellence.

As I mentioned previously, the body of Christ has been given the great responsibility to steward what God the Father has entrusted us to manage. Each believer will have to stand before the judgment seat of Christ to give a full account of what he was given to steward. (See Romans 14:10; 1 Corinthians 3:13; Revelation 22:12.) In the interim, the body of Christ has a lot of work to do as it pertains to stewardship. The Father is interested in the quality of our stewardship, and the quality of our stewardship is determined by the depth of our fellowship with God and the church. But we are falling behind in our duties as evidenced by the moral and ethical decay in the world. Hatred and confusion are rampant, world leaders cannot be trusted, and trouble and peril are on the rise as things continue to get worse. But God is calling the church to arise!

CHAPTER 1

Why We Need Order

GOD HAS A PLAN. His plan is to bring His church into divine alignment with His original plans and purposes for mankind and His kingdom here on Earth. Divine alignment means to walk in sync with God, according to Romans 12:1, which tells us to "present [our] bodies a living sacrifice, holy, acceptable unto God, which is [our] reasonable service" (KJV) and Galatians 5:22–23, which says we are to produce the fruit of the Spirit: "love, joy, peace, longsuffering, gentleness, goodness, faith, meekness, temperance: against such there is no law" (KJV). God has not changed His mind, and His truth marches on. Our job as Christians is to pray, turn from our wicked ways, and embrace God's truth (2 Chron. 7:14).

Writing about this topic isn't easy, but God has given me a mandate to bring to the forefront the lack of order in the church. God wants us to use the abilities He has given us to advance His kingdom, not to selfishly further our own agendas. Whenever we leave God out of the equation, our lives and pursuits end up in chaos. He is calling His church to return to her first love so that order can be restored.

Everything in the kingdom of God operates by love, for without love, nothing we do will work or prosper. The apostle Paul said:

> "If I speak with the tongues of men and of angels, but have not love, I am become sounding brass, or a clanging cymbal. And if I have the gift of prophecy, and know all mysteries and all knowledge; and if I have all faith, so as to remove mountains, but have not love, I am nothing. And if I bestow all my goods to feed the poor, and if I give my body [a]to be burned, but have not love, it profiteth me nothing" (1 Cor. 13:1–3, ASV).

Before God spoke and brought order out of chaos at creation, the earth was dark, empty, and shapeless. But when the Creator of the universe said, "Let there be light" (Gen. 1:3), there was light—and order.

So what is the meaning of order in relation to the modern church? Well-known televangelist Dr. Mike Murdock offers an astute definition in his teaching CD *7 Wisdom Keys for Organizing Your Life*: "Order is the accurate arrangement of things."

God designed order in heaven (the spiritual realm); in relationships (marriage, families, and professional and interpersonal relationships); systems (the world, governments, education), and in the earth (the kingdom of man, animal kingdom, and intergalactic kingdom).

It's Time to Get Real

Let's face it. The church is out of order, and whenever there is disorder, something is always jeopardized. Think about it this way. Dance partners must have one party designated to lead, right? If both partners try to lead and no one follows, someone inevitably will get out of step or even hurt.

Another example of disorder is found in James 1:8, which says "a double minded man is unstable in all his ways" (KJV). We can easily conclude that a "double mind" is a disordered and confused mind. A person in this state should not expect to receive anything from God (James 1:7). In order for the church to impact the world, our minds and hearts must be aligned and renewed daily with the Word of God.

Consider these key points:

1. We cannot mind the business of God with our minds because the church is God's idea. He is the sole owner and originator, and His ways are not our ways; His thoughts are not our thoughts. They are higher. (See Isaiah 55:8–9.)

2. The church was not created to be manipulated or governed by man or any other power that is inferior to God.

3. God entrusts men and women to offer servant-leadership in the church, not headship. Man is simply a steward and God is the Head.

Jesus Christ, the Bridegroom, is the owner and head of the church. He is the perfect prototype of how the church, which is known as the bride of Christ, should steward all the resources and responsibilities God has given us. Jesus said, "I must work the works of Him who sent Me, while it is day: the night cometh, when no man can work" (John 9:4, KJV). Jesus came to complete His Father's business on earth, and nothing, not even hell, would be able to stop Him. In much the same way, the body of Christ must be focused on what God has called us to do as individuals and collectively. He did not give the church time, talents, and gifts to waste. He gave us these resources to grow and mature us so we can impact the world for the kingdom of God. But first, we need divine order in the court—or in the church.

Understanding Protocol

From what I have concluded, protocol is the observance of and adherence to systematic instruction. It is a system of rules that explain or denote the correct conduct, process, and procedures to be followed that are specific to an environment. Protocol is the establishing and that are observance of order. It inspires a respect that produces honor, promotion, and unity in any given system.

We see an example of this in the Book of Esther. The second chapter, verse 12 says, "Now when every maid's turn was come to go in to king Ahasuerus, after that she had been twelve months, according to the manner of the women, (for so were the days of their purifications accomplished, to wit, six months with oil of myrrh, and six months with sweet odours, and with other things for the purifying of the women;)" (KJV). Esther had to undergo this tedious process of preparation before being presented to King Xerxes, also known as Ahasuerus. This passage in the Book of Esther illustrates that everything we do for God has requirements and protocols.

Merriam-Webster's dictionary defines protocol as "a code prescribing strict adherence to correct etiquette and precedence." The divinely ordered system that I call protocol was designed to protect and promote the presence of King Jesus. Protocol is also a means through which people respect and honor both divine and human authority. My overarching goal in this book is to teach Christians to understand and honor divine protocols so they can create the right

Stewarding the Anointing

environments for success and promotion through the power of the Holy Spirit.

Some protocols are observed and discerned while others are taught or documented for display. When I say documented for display, I'm referring to a display of words, pictures or symbols that describe or denote a systematic way of how something is to be done, i.e., signs are posted for people to see, or manuals are written for people to read. For instance, I love sandwiches and have been to nearly every sandwich chain in North Texas. One day I decided to visit a sandwich shop I had never been to. When I entered the sandwich shop, it was not clear to me where I should stand in line to order my food. I was also the only customer in the restaurant at the time, and there was no customer behavior to mimic. Because there were no visible or discernable protocols for that environment, I wasn't sure how to proceed. My only option was to ask the cashier for instructions. The lesson here is if you are unsure how to navigate a new environment, ask the host of that environment.

Once we understand the expected protocol, we can then align ourselves to the proper behavior. Let me explain a little further. If people don't understand the rules and regulations for an environment, order cannot be established or maintained. This can lead to chaos. It is best to document, demonstrate, or display the expected behavior. It's just like speed limits posted on streets and highways. Posted speed limits set velocity boundaries for drivers, and if they choose to disobey the law there will be dire consequences.

It is important to realize that protocol is a tool to be used to establish and maintain order in environments, not a weapon to wield against people. But in order to maintain a real sense of order there must be a guiding principle of protocol instead of a governing principle of protocol.

Guiding protocols empower people, but governing protocols enslave people.

Many people who work and serve in ministry shun the mere mention of the word *protocol* because it's been misunderstood by too many church leaders who used rules and regulations to lord over people instead of liberating them through a mutually beneficial relationship. This misguided, governing misuse of systematic protocol is legalism at its best, and it enslaves people. Rules must be motivated by relationship so there will be commitment to follow-ship. God, our loving Father, is the Master at inviting a person to enter into a relationship with Him first. Then He becomes their Shepherd to guide them along their journey to grow as a Christian. If we are to truly walk with God, we must do things His way.

The following passage of Scripture offers a balanced picture of the difference between rules and relationship, which are both are necessary:

> "Not that we are sufficient of ourselves to think anything as of ourselves; but our sufficiency is of God; who also hath made us able ministers of the new testament; not of the letter, but of the spirit: for the letter killeth, but the spirit giveth life." (2 Cor. 3: 5–6, KJV).

In the kingdom of God, every protocol is met and supported by the anointing—the supernatural-enabling power of God. Because Christians have been anointed by the Holy Spirit, we can pray for the sick and see them recover, as stated in James 5: 14-16:

> "Is anyone among you sick? Let them call the elders of the church to pray over them and anoint them with oil in the name of the Lord. And the prayer offered in faith will make the sick person well; the

Lord will raise them up. If they have sinned, they will be forgiven" (NIV).

Whenever the people of God pray, the anointing is there to yield explosive results. On the other hand, where there is disorder or disunity, there is no anointing for great exploits. God does not and will not sanction His anointing when there's division of heart and ill purpose. I will discuss the anointing in more detail in an upcoming chapter.

A Perfect Partnership

To execute our assignments, roles, and duties in life—be it our responsibility to family, work, or ministry—we must understand that protocol and stewardship are inseparable partners. Any operation void of this pair would result in a failed mission. We, the church, must adhere to God's divine order of stewardship.

It is important to observe the protocol for a given situation and exercise proper stewardship (or what to do) for that same assignment. The protocol will vary according to the assignment at hand. Keep in mind, protocol is the direct instruction for construction. For instance, before you build anything or start a project, it is important to understand the instructions. Protocol is the grace given to successfully execute the instruction. Glory to God!

When it comes to divine order, we must recognize that just as truth and grace are married so are protocol and stewardship. Take another look at the following scripture: "Who also hath made us able ministers of the new testament; not of the letter, but of the spirit: for the letter killeth, but the spirit giveth life" (2 Cor. 3:6, KJV). Just as the letter alone kills, protocol alone is detrimental to a person who is attempting to carry out their God-given assignment.

Some leaders abuse their subordinates in the name of protocol. They attempt to control them with written or verbal recitations of the rules and regulations, much like the Pharisees did to Jesus. They stress the rules but ignore or don't even realize the need for relationship.

When people feel bombarded with rules, they can be motivated by fear to get a job done, and that is counter-productive. People should not be made to feel they can never make a mistake, nor should they be punished when they do. Humans make mistakes. A problem arises when leaders have not made the effort to build relationships with the people whom God put "on loan" to them. Instead, they take on an ownership and superior mindset and end up treating their subordinates like slaves. Perhaps it's because they lack interpersonal skills, or maybe their leadership skills are altogether lacking.

Leaders who assume the role of owner instead of steward treat people like slaves and thus become abusers. When this happens, it is stewardship gone wrong. Protocol alone pronounces judgment and does not allow room for error. But protocol coupled with stewardship produces truth and grace to carry out the assignment at hand and makes room for recovery when mistakes are made. In an article at the Houston Chronicle website, writer Beth Rifkin defines protocol this way: "Protocols and procedures are the specific way that a policy, rule or principle is carried out. It can often be thought of as a set of instructions." My definition of stewardship is the administration of a gift, or resource management; whereas protocol gives you the operational instructions for what you've been called to manage or steward. The how to (protocol) must be set in place before administering the what to (stewardship).

The movie *The Devil Wears Prada* is a great demonstration of how protocol and stewardship work together. The frumpy assistant who shows up to her new job in the high-fashion industry is totally clueless and carefree about the office dress code and proper decorum. No thanks to the reluctant aid of a few of her coworkers, this assistant received the *how to* and the *what to do* of her assignment. They gave her a crash course about the fashion industry, how to dress, and how to cater to the "big boss." The emergency assistance she received enabled her to keep her job and win a promotion to travel with their difficult boss to Paris, France. The assistant's observance and strict adherence to the systems in place at her job ultimately set her up for favor with her boss. What is my point? If you want favor and promotion in your life, practice the kingdom principles of protocol (information) and stewardship (application).

CHAPTER 2

Who Is the Church?

BEFORE WE DISCUSS the actual function of the church, we must first review her purpose. The church is a body of believers engaged in an intimate, corporate relationship with Jesus. The church was born on the day of Pentecost when about one hundred and twenty men and women were gathered in the Upper Room and were filled with the Holy Spirit, according to Acts 1:15; Acts 2:1–4.

Even though the Holy Spirit was introduced in the Upper Room, that doesn't mean Christians are to confine themselves to a building. The church is not a temperature-gauged tomb of high-tech tools or a fancy arena where people gather together. She's a living, breathing organism, designed to *re-present* Christ to the world to the glory of God. Christ is risen, and therefore the church is risen.

Christ completed the work and sat down at the right hand of the Father, but not before He commissioned the church to rise up and be about the Father's business. The church is the equipping ground and launching pad for the saints of the Most High God. Christ told Peter, "Upon this rock I will build my church; and the gates of hell shall not prevail against it" (Matt. 16:18, KJV). Considering my previous statement about the church being an equipping and launching pad, no member of Christ's body should ever be released into ministry until he or she has a firm foundation. Believers are anointed by God, but they must be properly equipped and then launched by leadership. Why? Because God desires to develop character in believers before releasing them.

What is character, you might ask? Character is credibility with God. It means God can trust you. Character development comes through an abiding relationship with Christ, coupled with accountability to leadership. As we develop and maintain a keen awareness of God's presence through an intimate relationship with Christ, our behavior will be governed by our love for Him.

Character development is a crucial component as believers mature in their giftings. The believer's character is developed inwardly and it directly impacts outward behavior. We must be careful to display character and not foolish behavior because God is looking to release crowns, not clowns. He wants His church to demonstrate His glory to the world.

God anoints and appoints those He has called. To be anointed is to receive God's stamp of approval. From a worldly standpoint, people can anoint people- meaning, they can put their own stamp of approval on someone, apart from God's choosing or His Blessing, as is illustrated in many Old Testament stories. In 1 Samuel 8, the people of Israel wanted their own king, and God granted them their wish: But when they said, "Give us a king to lead us," this displeased Samuel, so he prayed to the Lord. And the Lord told him:

> "Listen to all that the people are saying to you; it is not you they have rejected, but they have rejected me as their king. As they have done from the day I brought them up out of Egypt until this day, forsaking me and serving other gods, so they are doing to you. Now listen to them; but warn them solemnly and let them know what the king who will reign over them will claim as his rights"' (vv. 7–9, NIV).

Based on my previous definition above, when people anoint someone God did not approve of, they will many times seek to own or control that person because of greed, selfishness, prestige, power, etc. Some people believe because they have promoted you or given you an opportunity, they own you- it's a sense of entitlement. And, even when God sends someone He anointed as a steward for an assignment, people can still try to control or assume ownership of that person's life for the same reasons.

Whether someone "went" or was "sent" by God on assignment, leaders who have an ownership mentality are likely to impose unreasonable demands on their worker's personal time, work schedules, so much so that the person loses sight of a proper personal life balance. I must note that this type of leadership is enslavement and bondage, and those who fall prey to it must refocus their attention and passion towards God, not on a person or the work of the ministry.

It is critical that we recognize God as our only source and everything and everyone else as merely a resource. We cannot impact the kingdom of God by being preoccupied with wanting our own way or receiving approval from the world system (the world, the flesh, and the devil).

The world will be confounded and even outraged by how God moves His kingdom forward, but the church must not be afraid of the persecution or disapproval of the world. We must look to please the Lord and seek His approval at all costs. We will experience His manifest presence when we submit to His will and way.

The church must recognize that "every good gift and every perfect gift is from above, and cometh down from the Father of lights, with whom is no variableness, neither shadow of turning" (James 1:17, KJV). Once we realize that, we can begin to recognize and honor the gifts and talents God has given us. But everything He has given us is in seed form. It is our responsibility to nurture the seeds and cultivate the garden of our assignment. This is a critical process. This is why the church is so important.

Equipping the Saints

Ephesians 4 outlines the importance of unity and maturity in the body of Christ. The following passage of Scripture describes the purpose of the body of Christ:

> "And he gave some, apostles; and some, prophets; and some, evangelists; and some, pastors and teachers; for the perfecting of the saints, for the work of the ministry, for the edifying of the body of Christ" (Eph. 4:11–12, KJV).

Every member of the body of Christ, if he or she is to be a change agent for the kingdom of God, must have a firm foundation of God's truth and be linked into an accountability system. This ensures proper launching and safety as the members travel throughout the globe on behalf of the kingdom. God did not call the church to the four walls of a building; He called her to the four corners of the earth!

In Scripture, the church is referred to in the feminine gender because she is the bride of Christ. Christ, the Bridegroom, died and sacrificed His life for her. Jesus demonstrated the perfect model of marriage for man and wife while He lived on earth by dying sacrificially for the church. Ephesians 5:25 makes the point, "Husbands, love your wives, just as Christ loved the church and gave himself up for her" (NIV).

While I'm on the marriage topic I will reinforce this truth: Christ's model of marriage is one man and one woman joined together in holy matrimony, "God is not human, that he should lie, not a human being, that he should change his mind. Does he speak and then not act? Does he promise and not fulfill?" (Num. 23:19, NIV). This means that God does not and will not change His mind about His plan for marriage. God's Word is settled. Though the world is ever-changing, Jesus Christ remains the same today, yesterday, and forevermore.

There are misguided notions among Christians and people in the world about what the church is and what she should look like. Many believe God's work can only be done in or at a building, and this belief is solely based on what some have experienced, seen or heard. Oftentimes, I have had to deal with comments and wise cracks from people I know who do not go to church, but they know I do.

One person told me, "Aren't you home early from church? I expected you to be there all day today." Here's another statement someone made to me when I was eating leftover barbeque in an employee break room at work after a Memorial Day holiday, "Did the church barbeque?" I laughed at both scenarios for a moment, but then I realized how distorted the view is of the church.

The church has created and perpetuated the misconception that ministry only takes place in a physical building because she has not influenced society beyond the four walls. And, of course, those who have been negatively acquainted with the church want nothing to do with it. I find it deeply concerning how many people outside the church view those who are in the church. Many have been verbally abused, judged, criticized, and even ostracized by people purporting to be Christians (and perhaps they are). As a result, too many people want nothing to do with the church. And I understand why they feel that way.

The church has much cleaning up to do. The work must begin at home and spread out into the world. Hear ye! Hear ye! Christ has mobile units He wants to deploy. Christians have been sitting down in the church so long that many have become chickens which have wings but live their lives on the ground, never leaving the coop, rather than eagles, which mount up with wings and soar to great heights. And yes, this is a wake-up call for the church to get in her rightful place and mobilize her units!

By the time you finish reading this book, I hope you will be persuaded to act. It is my prayer that both the church and the world would have an accurate view of Christ and His body, but it's not going to happen until believers arise! I pray that the church will soon recognize, embrace, and employ her call to impact the world so that the world through Christ can be saved.

Every member of the church has been given gifts and talents. I pray that the church will not marvel at the gifts but magnify the Giver by putting those gifts to work for His glory alone. I pray that members of the body of Christ will not sit on the sidelines and limit their scope to thinking only a few are meant to walk in the gifts listed in Ephesians 4. Rather, I pray they realize if we look to Christ, He will do the marvelous and miraculous through us, His body, which is lacking nothing. We have one Lord, one faith, one baptism, and we are one body of believers.

I pray that "instead, speaking the truth in love, we will grow to become in every respect the mature body of him who is the head, that is, Christ. From him the whole body, joined and held together by every supporting ligament, grows and builds itself up in love, as each part does its work" (Eph. 4:15–16, NIV). Whereas, all the members of Christ's church are fitly joined together. And we know all things work together for the good of them who love the Lord, and who are the called according to His purpose. In Jesus' name I pray, Amen.

Remember, love is what keeps us together. Realize the church is a body, a living and breathing organism, not a building. First Corinthians 12:12 says, "For even as the body is one and yet has many members, and all the members of the body, though they are many, are one body, so also is Christ" (NASB).

CHAPTER 3

The Anointing

THROUGHOUT THE BIBLE, we read about the anointing—what it is and why it matters to the believer. Understanding the anointing is important because I believe it is impossible to be impactful for the kingdom without this knowledge. The question at hand is, What is the anointing? The anointing is the Spirit of Christ Jesus in the Person of the Holy Spirit:

> "The Spirit of the LORD is upon Me, because He anointed Me to preach the Gospel to the poor. He has sent Me to proclaim release to the captives, and recovery of sight to the blind, to set free those who are oppressed, to proclaim the favorable year of the LORD" (Luke 4:18, NASB).

In Isaiah 10:27, the Lord's people who dwelled in Zion were under attack by the Assyrians but because of the anointing, the burden and the yoke were removed from God's people. The anointing provides supernatural enablement, but who carries it? At the point of salvation, the Holy Spirit indwells every born-again believer who has professed Christ Jesus as Lord and Savior and every believer can access the anointing through the power and presence of the Holy Spirit.

Among the greatest privileges we have as Christians is the privilege to become one with God and to be endowed with His supernatural, enabling power, the anointing. This supernatural ability emanates from the Holy Spirit of God. The anointing empowers Christians to carry out all the Father has called and commanded them to do. And because of Christ, the Anointed One, we know we can do all things through Him who gives us strength (Phil. 4:13).

Because of the anointing, Christians can perform great exploits for God's kingdom. We read in Judges 15:14–16 that God gave Samson the power to defeat the Philistines who came to kill him while he was bound: "When he [Samson] came to Lehi, the Philistines came shouting against him. Then the Spirit of the Lord came mightily upon him; and the ropes that were on his arms became like flax that is burned with fire, and his bonds broke loose from his hands. He found a fresh jawbone of a donkey, reached out his hand and took it, and killed a thousand men with it. Then Samson said: 'With the jawbone of a donkey, heaps upon heaps, with the jawbone of a donkey I have slain a thousand men!'" (NKJV). What a great exploit! God enabled Samson to sorely defeat his enemies.

This same supernatural enabling ability (the anointing) has been made available to us today as children of the Most High God. We can rest confidently in knowing "when the enemy comes in like a flood, the Spirit of the Lord will lift up a standard against him" (Isa. 59:19, NKJV).

Christians today have the power of God on loan. God empowers us by His Spirit, not to do what we want but to do according to God's plans. We, therefore, must be mindful that the power of God is at work in us so that we don't try to take credit for what God is doing or has done. Philippians 2:13 says, "For it is God which worketh in you both to will and to do of his good pleasure" (KJV). We must not mistake God's supernatural enabling ability with our human ability. Put another way, the glory can touch you, but don't you touch the glory—it belongs solely to God. Man is simply a conduit. God is the "Can do it," "Will do it," and "Did it"!

John 15:5 states that man can do nothing without God: "I am the vine, ye are the branches: He that abideth in me, and I in him, the same bringeth forth much fruit: for without me ye can do nothing" (KJV). This verse describes Jesus, who is the Vine, as the lifeline to the body of Christ, which is referred to as the branches. The Vine sustains the branches; without the Vine the branches cannot thrive.

In order to understand how the anointing is activated and how we can be good stewards of the anointing, we must first understand the term *unity*. *Unity* implies a oneness, a coming together, an agreement about how something is to be done and/or how something or someone is to function. Philippians 2:2 outlines the will of Christ for His church to be united: "Fulfil ye my joy, that ye be likeminded, having the same love, being of one accord, of one mind" (KJV).

Let's also recount what happened in the Upper Room on the day of Pentecost in Acts 2:1–4: "When the day of Pentecost came, they were all together in one place. Suddenly a sound like the blowing of a violent wind came from heaven and filled the whole house where they were sitting. They saw what seemed to be tongues of fire that separated and came to rest on each of them. All of them were filled with the Holy Spirit and began to speak in other tongues as the Spirit enabled them" (NIV).

Let me set the stage for what happened in Acts 2:1–4. The conditions in the Upper Room were highly conducive for a mighty move of God because the people were praying in one accord. They were in one place, and suddenly the

Holy Spirit showed up. When the Holy Spirit showed up, the anointing showed up. And whenever the anointing breaks forth, men become supernaturally empowered to do what they were incapable of doing before. And when that happened in Acts 2, "suddenly" there was an explosive expansion of the church. The Bible says about three thousand souls were added to the church that day (Acts 2:41).

What a stellar example of how the anointing is activated when there's unity of heart, mind, purpose, and function. When members of the body of Christ operate in one accord, the King of glory shall come in. The Lord God strong and mighty takes over.

The Purpose of the Anointing

The anointing is the "unction to function." Again, this supernatural enablement comes from the presence and power of the Holy Spirit. One of His functions is to impart the God-apportioned grace to function in a God-ordained assignment. Simply stated, the Holy Spirit equips and empowers believers with gifts and abilities to do God's work here on earth. When the Holy Spirit indwells us, He gives us supernatural gifts. First Corinthians 12 details the spiritual gifts the Holy Spirit has given to believers to equip the body of Christ for the work of the ministry:

> There are different kinds of gifts, but the same Spirit distributes them. There are different kinds of service, but the same Lord. —1 CORINTHIANS 12:4–5, NIV

When God calls believers, He appoints them for a specific role and provides them with a specific anointing to fulfill that assignment. When God chose David to be king over Israel, he sent Samuel the prophet to anoint him:

> "And Samuel said to Jesse, 'Are all the young men here?' Then he said, 'There remains yet the youngest, and there he is, keeping the sheep.' And Samuel said to Jesse, 'Send and bring him. For we will not sit down till he comes here.' So he sent and brought him in. Now he was ruddy, with bright eyes, and good-looking. And the Lord said, 'Arise, anoint him; for this is the one!' Then Samuel took the horn of oil and anointed him in the midst of his brothers; and the Spirit of the Lord came upon David from that day forward" (I Sam. 16:11–13, NKJV).

As Bible teacher W. H. Westcott wrote, "The anointing not only marked him out for the position but conferred upon him the necessary power and fitness to be and to walk in every way worthy of the position for which he was designated."

With the anointing of the Holy Spirit, the body of Christ is equipped to perform great exploits for God's kingdom here on earth. Conversely, without the anointing of the Holy Spirit, believers lack the supernatural enablement to carry out the work of the kingdom. Jesus told His disciples, "Verily, verily, I say unto you, He that believeth on me, the works that I do shall he do also; and greater works than these shall he do; because I go unto my Father" (John 14:12, KJV). When Jesus returned to the Father, He sent the Holy Spirit to dwell in and among the body of Christ to help achieve God's purposes and plans in the earth.

The anointing is for service in a divine assignment. The assignment is specific to the individual, and the anointing is specific for that assignment. To explain further, let's say you have a prescription to pick-up from the drug store. How will you identify your prescription? Most likely the following will be on the bottle of medication: your name and address, the name of the medicine, a list of possible side effects, and instructions on how to administer the exact dosage. The anointing is much like a prescription, and it is based on the Father's prognosis for a given situation or circumstance. The prescribed anointing, when activated, treats the problem and as a result, the symptoms will go away.

The anointing is designed to provide a prescribed unction to function, and it specifically addresses dysfunctions such as bondage, fear, anxiety, sickness and disease. For every issue or circumstance, there is an anointing given to every believer for that situation through the power of the Holy Spirit. If someone is sick, there is an anointing for healing. For financial difficulties, there is an anointing for wisdom; if someone is depressed, there's an anointing of joy.

Having the power of God means freedom from all forms of bondage is possible—God's power flows through His anointing. So when you find yourself in a situation too big for you to handle, look to God to be your helper and deliverer.

Jesus Paid the Ultimate Price

Jesus paid a high price for the anointing. In fact, the anointing cost Jesus His life. He paid this price in full when He shed His blood on the cross, and in order to walk in His anointing we must be willing to lay our lives down too. The anointing will even cost you your life in one form or another. Every believer will pay a price for the Spirit-graced anointing. Face it, it costs to be you. God's calling on your life could mean the loss of your way of doing things; moving out of the state or country; alienation from family members; or the loss of a relationship, status, finances, and more. But remember, that loss is gain in God's economy. As the apostle

Paul wrote, "For to me to live is Christ, and to die is gain" (Phil. 1:21, KJV). You will be rewarded for what you are willing to lose for Christ's sake. If you are not willing to lose the thing God wants you to sacrifice, you will lose it anyway, and there will be no gain. Again, Paul said it best: "What is more, I consider everything a loss because of the surpassing worth of knowing Christ Jesus my Lord, for whose sake I have lost all things. I consider them garbage, that I may gain Christ" (Phil. 3:8, NIV).

A major part of the preparation for your call may be trial by fire. Jesus told us we would have trouble in the world but to be of good cheer because He has overcome the world (John 16:33). Peter wrote, "Beloved, do not be surprised at the fiery trial when it comes upon you to test you, as though something strange were happening to you. But rejoice insofar as you share Christ's sufferings, that you may also rejoice and be glad when his glory is revealed" (1 Pet. 4:12–13, ESV).

Just as olives are crushed to produce oil, God uses trials to produce the anointing in the body of Christ. Once the vessel is crushed, the oil of brokenness spills out and runs down. The oil is designed to flow from the head of the church, which is Christ, to the body of Christ. When filled to the point of overflowing, the vessels, which represent believers, spill over to other vessels. When the anointing bursts forth, there is enough oil to go around, and then some.

Here is another practical example of how the anointing works. I would liken it to oil in a car engine. The oil is designed to help the engine run smoothly. In fact, engine oil keeps all affiliated parts engaged and working properly. On the other hand, if there is no oil in the engine, the engine will fail and the car will not be drivable.

How can we represent God with no oil in our engine? If this happens, we will be rendered ineffective. The question then becomes, How do we get our oil back? We must exert some effort. The anointing oil can be produced in various ways, including through praise, worship, repentance, obedience, love, purity, and forgiveness. The list is not exhaustive. Employ these elements in your everyday life and watch the oil flow. Psalm 133 declares: "Behold, how good and how pleasant it is for brethren to dwell together in unity! It is like the precious ointment upon the head, that ran down upon the beard, even Aaron's beard: that went down to the skirts of his garments; for there the Lord commanded the blessing, even life for evermore" (KJV).

The fiery trials of your life can never be too hot for God to enter because He is the all-consuming fire. He consumes the fire, not you. Just ask Shadrach, Meshach, and Abednego, the three young Hebrew men who were saved in the midst of the fiery furnace in Daniel chapter 3. The three men were fired by the king, but they were "puri-fired" by God for service. You will be tried in the fire, and through the process you will be purified for His call on your life. Then and only then will He smear His mark, the anointing, of approval on you for a specific assignment. And God will equip whom He strips. He will not share His glory, nor will He compete with idols or the gods some people erect in their lives, knowingly or unknowingly.

The Hebrew term mashach, which is translated "anointing," means "to smear, anoint, spread a liquid." Although it is a New Testament account, this is the action referenced in Matthew 26:6–13 (KJV), which details how Jesus was prepared for His burial:

> Now when Jesus was in Bethany, in the house of Simon the leper, there came unto him a woman having an alabaster box of very precious ointment, and poured it on his head, as he sat at meat. But when his disciples saw it, they had indignation, saying, To what purpose is this waste? For this ointment might have been sold for much and given to the poor. When Jesus understood it, he said unto them, Why trouble ye the woman? for she hath wrought a good work upon me. For ye have the poor always with you; but me ye have not always. For in that she hath poured this ointment on my body, she did it for my burial. Verily I say unto you, Wheresoever this gospel shall be preached in the whole world, there shall also this, that this woman hath done, be told for a memorial of her.

As believers, we must not mistake the anointing with a feeling or chill bumps. It is the power of God in full demonstration. A person might have feelings and chill bumps as a result of experiencing the anointing, but these are not necessarily indications that the anointing is present.

When miracles, signs, and wonders take place, God's power is clearly at work. People being healed from an incurable disease, and receiving financial miracles, and answered prayer are also signs that God's power is at work. The anointing always yields freedom, major victory, and joy. Simply put, the anointing makes things easy. It is the oil in the engine that helps the vehicle run smoothly. We are the engine, and God's Spirit is the oil. Always remember, God doesn't need our efforts; He needs our cooperation. When we allow Him to work through us as willing and yielded vessels, He will do the impossible. Praise Him!

CHAPTER 4

Management of the Anointing

IT IS YOUR RESPONSIBILITY as a believer to discover the anointings with which you have been graced. Pay attention to the areas in your life where you dominate, or bring freedom, healing, revelation, and deliverance. You must become familiar with the areas God designated you to manage and take over for His name's sake.

How do you find the anointing God has graced you with? The first step is to find your place in a relationship with God. Everything He does is based on relationship. He desires that everyone know Him, not just know *of* Him. I can attest that to know Him is to truly love Him. How do you get to know someone? Well, in specific relational terms, you must spend quality time with the person, communicate with the person, and learn the person's likes and dislikes. When it comes to an intimate relationship, you must learn to be vulnerable with the person. Get naked. Yes, you read that correctly—get naked, meaning take off all masks, facades, or anything else that might hinder intimacy with God.

In a true, loving relationship there is intimacy. There is trust, safety, and sharing of private information that leaves you vulnerable. Real intimacy is designed to make you feel safe, not ashamed. If you don't feel safe being naked in an intimate relationship, you might need to put your clothes back on, guard your heart, and step away from that intimate space. Run if you have to!

Speaking of being naked, you may recall that in 2 Samuel 6:14 David danced in the presence of God wearing nothing but a linen ephod after the ark of the covenant was returned to Jerusalem. What pure joy! As David demonstrated, we enter the truest and purest form of intimacy when we can dance naked and uninhibited in the presence of God. This is what I call worship. This is what God desires of believers.

In order to know true intimacy, you must first learn how to be intimate with God. He knows you and loves you more than anyone ever could. If you don't learn how to be intimate with God, then your level of intimacy and functionality in all other relationships will be severely limited.

Finding Your Fit

Now, on to the next step to finding your place in God. You must be trained to walk in-step with the Holy Spirit. What does this mean? This means you must cultivate a relationship with the Holy Spirit through Jesus our Lord. How can two walk together in unity lest they agree? (See Amos 3:3.) The Holy Spirit is the best mentor we could ever have. He is our Helper, Teacher, and Keeper. We cannot properly manage what belongs to God without the aid of the Holy Spirit. Let the Holy Spirit lead and guide you as you walk with Him.

Once you identify and operate in the areas of your gifting—whether it is singing, speaking, writing, doctoring, or serving in some other ministry or work setting—it will become noticeable. Your leaders and co-laborers in ministry will begin to point out the difference and impact you bring whenever you operate in your particular gift(s). Keep in mind, as you begin to exercise the power vested in you, you will become responsible for managing it appropriately.

Managing the anointing appropriately means living a consecrated lifestyle. Anointed people are set apart by God. Stewards of the anointing are peculiar and cannot do or live the way the world does. Holy living can be a narrow-gated, lonely lifestyle. Matthew 7:13–14 says, "Enter through the narrow gate. For wide is the gate and broad is the road that leads to destruction, and many enter through it. But small is the gate and narrow the road that leads to life, and only a few find it" (NIV).

The wide gate holds a wide crowd. But remember, Christ walked the lonely, narrow road to Calvary to sacrifice His life for all.

Paying the Price

Managing the anointing also includes protecting the call of God on your life. It means maintaining an uncontaminated vessel. Believers are Christ's vessels of honor, and maintaining a pure anointing requires a lifestyle of holiness, purity, and repentance; constant fellowship with God; and a keen sensitivity to the Holy Spirit so as not to grieve Him, as mentioned in the previous chapter. This means protecting what you see, hear, speak, and do, and watching the company you keep.

The price of the anointing is very steep, and with that price comes the great sacrifice of time, relationships, obedience, service, and more—that is, if we wish to maintain a great grace of the anointing in our lives. The question then becomes, How bad do you want to be anointed? Bear in mind that the anointing is not just for church; it's for work and every aspect of your life as a Christian. God has given believers His "power on loan," as the saying goes, and we are to appropriate the anointing in every area of our lives. The anointing, when stewarded appropriately, will always yield new life, sweatless victories, and great exploits for the kingdom of God.

Mismanaging the Anointing

One cannot experience the manifest presence and power of God in a place or state of disorder and discord. Order must be established. For every God-given assignment, there is a divine instruction. For every gift, there is an administrative process and an anointing that comes with employing that gift. For example, I am a soloist. A singer has a musical accompanist and a choir director when backed by a choir. The choir has its set of instructions, and so do the soloist and accompanist. The instructions for that assignment must be communicated and adhered to by everyone; otherwise there will be chaos. Any deviation from the order of God will greatly diminish an experience with God, lead to confusion, and even cause harm.

At times I have been guilty of mismanaging the grace of God upon my life, specifically the gifts I have been given. God made me a giver, and in giving I have given too much to the wrong people. Many times I gave when I was depleted emotionally and financially. This mismanagement cost me time, emotional turmoil, and at times a loss of my sense of self. Even though I have been graced with an anointing to give to and do for others, that same gift worked against me when I misappropriated that gift and allowed someone else to misuse the gift. We must be Spirit-filled and Spirit-led in our giving so that we can give out of an abundance and not from a deficit. We must also understand that everything God has commissioned us to steward has been assigned to a designated time, place, person(s), and proportion. It is our job to discern when, how, and to what degree God wants to use us in a given assignment.

There is such a thing as giving too much or going overboard, or frankly just doing too much! Need I say more? It is possible to give too much time and attention to others or to things. You may not be one to frivolously give away money, but perhaps you have given too much of your time, energy, counsel, and most of all your heart to people without taking the time to care for yourself and guard your heart in the process. We have all lacked wisdom at one time or another, much like Joseph when his brothers threw him into a pit because he shared his dream with them. Joseph did not guard his heart, and it nearly cost him his life. We must learn to qualify people for our hearts because we have an enemy out there that wants to destroy our lives.

There are some people who have been sent on assignment by the devil to try to rob us of the very thing God placed in our hearts the desire to do. Therefore, we must be sober, vigilant, and careful about who we share our dreams with, because when you share your dreams you share your heart. Proverbs 4:23 says, "Above all else, guard your heart, for everything you do flows from it" (NIV). When we share our hearts irresponsibly, we mismanage the anointing on our lives.

Exercising stewardship without wisdom is recklessness. When we don't exercise proper stewardship, we will frivolously and carelessly mishandle God's property. Just because you have been given a gift doesn't mean you should share it with any and everyone. Now, we all seem to know that is true when it comes to money, but what about when it comes to sharing your dreams, secret desires, family drama, or childhood traumas? When we give this type of information to people who cannot properly manage or keep it private, we invite shipwreck into our lives because the enemy will use this information to gain an advantage over us and try to destroy us. We must understand that there are always spies in the land, so beware.

In general, people mishandle what they don't understand. The late Dr. Myles Munroe once said, "When purpose is not known, abuse is inevitable." When we give information to people who are not properly equipped to handle our precious jewels, or if we are that person who is irresponsible with our own treasures, it will always create havoc. It's like casting pearls before swine—you will be trampled upon. This type of havoc can and should be averted at all costs.

We must learn to use wisdom when sharing our heart with others, because not everyone deserves to know your innermost being. There's nothing that says a person is automatically qualified to know your heart. But there should be such a thing as automatic disqualification when we discover someone cannot be trusted. Some people are unfit for your life, or for an area of your life, and you must govern yourself accordingly. No one should ever automatically qualify to access your heart but God. Everyone else must be tested and tried.

Learn to keep some of the things God shares with you private, meaning solely between you and Him. This is what intimacy with the Father is all about. Ask God for wisdom about what to share and what not to share because there are some things that He wants to share with you and you alone.

Keep in mind that it is not always safe to share heart secrets, even with the people closest to you. The enemy is always looking for a loophole to destroy you, and he will try to use those closest to you. God has given each of us gifts, and it is our responsibility to properly steward these gifts with His divine direction and wisdom. If you are guilty of mismanagement, simply repent and ask God to give you wisdom concerning your heart so you can walk in victory.

CHAPTER 5

Activating the Anointing

NOW THAT WE KNOW more about the anointing, let's look at how it can be activated for use in the kingdom of God! Christians are endowed with the power of Christ through the gift of the Holy Spirit at the point of salvation. Oftentimes, Christians don't know how to use that power. I am certain you can agree that there's nothing worse than having a prized possession and not know how to use it. For instance, a parked Ferrari is of no use without gas in the tank and a key to put in the ignition. Lord have mercy! Once we begin to understand how to function under the anointing, we will become better equipped to steward the power God has given us.

The anointing is designed to set all captives free from any and all forms of bondage and suffering. When the Spirit of the Lord is present, liberty is guaranteed, as referenced in

2 Corinthians 3:17, "Now the LORD is the Spirit, and where the Spirit of the LORD is, there is freedom" (NIV).

In order for the anointing to be activated or set in motion, certain conditions must be in place. Whether you're alone with Christ or among two or more individuals, His Presence is there with you, and where the Spirit of the Lord is there is liberty. Jesus said in Matthew 18:19–20:

"Again I say unto you, That if two of you shall agree on earth as touching any thing that they shall ask, it shall be done for them of my Father which is in heaven. For where two or three are gathered together in my name, there am I in the midst of them" (KJV).

Faith is an action word and an active command. Jesus commanded His followers to have faith in Him. Not wish, hope, or expect—He said to have faith. Faith is actively believing what God has promised. Dr. Tony Evans said, "Faith is acting like it is so, even when it is not so, so that it might be so, simply because God said so." A faith-filled environment will surely activate the anointing. "So then faith cometh by hearing, and hearing by the word of God" (Rom. 10:17, KJV).

Another component to unleashing the anointing is strict adherence to a divine instruction, which is obedience. A divine instruction is an explicit directive given by God that is designed to facilitate His direct involvement in the problem at hand. When we obey God-given directives, supernatural breakthroughs and miracles occur. John 2: 1–11 details the account of a wedding in Cana in Galilee where Jesus performed the miracle of turning water into wine. Just before Jesus performed this miracle, He gave two consecutive divine instructions to the servants at the wedding. His first instruction was, "Fill the jars with water" (verse 7, NIV). Once the servants followed through with the first instruction, Jesus gave the second instruction in verse 8: "Now draw some out and take it to the master of the feast" (NIV). The servants obeyed Jesus' instructions and it resulted in a miracle.

God provides divine instructions to prepare people for a move of God in various settings and crisis situations. It is important to note that divine instructions cannot be rationalized because they do not make sense to the natural mind. When God gives a divine instruction, our comprehension is never a prerequisite for obedience. He wants us to just obey Him and not try to figure things out. I've experienced situations where God told me to apologize to someone I knew I hadn't wronged. It made no sense to me at the time, but when I apologized, I saw how God used my apology to open the person's heart to receive His love and compassion.

The Bible is replete with examples of miracles that took place when people carried out God's divine instructions– Jesus feeding the multitude with two fish and five loaves of bread; the miracle of the widow at Zarephath; Moses and the children of Israel being saved from the Egyptians at the Red Sea, and the healing of Naaman the leper, who dipped himself seven times in the Dead Sea. There are many, many more accounts, and I'm certain you can also testify about the miracles God has performed in your life.

Now that we better understand how to activate the anointing, we must be careful not to be a hindrance to the anointing. When we grieve the Spirit with things such as unbelief, discord, disobedience, and all sorts of sin, it can hinder a move of God. It is our reasonable service as Christians to properly steward the anointing, the oh so precious super-enabling power meted to us by the grace of God.

Stewarding the Anointing

There is an anointing for every God-purposed work. This means God has already enabled us to do what He purposed us to do. God knew we could not do what He called us to do without Him. That's why He sent Jesus, and that's why Jesus gave us the Comforter to work within us. Because the Holy Spirit is at work in us, it is our responsibility as stewards of the anointing to keep our temples clean, healthy, and well-oiled through prayer and repentance. Maintaining the temple of God is our stewardship duty. Our bodies and everything else that was made all belong to God, "For ye are bought with a price: therefore glorify God in your body, and in your spirit, which are God's" (1 Cor. 6:20, KJV).

God has graced the body of Christ with the great responsibility of stewardship, and the best part is the Holy Spirit comes alongside us to assist us in carrying out great exploits for the kingdom. Jesus purposed the church to be empowered by the Holy Spirit, who would enable us to do even greater works than He did, according to John 14:12, "Verily, verily, I say unto you, He that believeth on me, the works that I do shall he do also; and greater works than these shall he do; because I go unto my Father" (KJV).

Stewarding the anointing also involves practicing the presence of God. This requires effort and intention on our part. When we become sensitive to God's presence through the person of the Holy Spirit, we aim to be still and abide, which is to hang out with Him. After we spend time with Him, our motives change from wanting something from Him to knowing something about Him.

When we practice God's presence, He teaches us to love what He loves and hate what He hates. Our obedience is the byproduct of getting to know Him. To know Him is to love

Him, and when we love Him we will obey Him. Jesus said in John 14:15, "If you love Me, keep My commandments" (NKJV).

Oftentimes, I practice the presence of God while reading the Word. As I spend time in the Word, whether reading it aloud or singing psalms of praise, I immediately sense the presence of the Lord fill the room. God always watches over His Word to perform it, so if you want Him to show up, speak His Word. Let's strive to hang out with God to get to know His voice, His Word, His character, and most of all, His love for us.

Once we become more acquainted with God by practicing His presence, we will endeavor to protect His presence. You may be wondering, How do we protect the presence of God? By watching what our mouth speaks, what our eyes see, and what our ears hear. When we desire to live in God's presence, we will become more sensitized to what makes Him leave the room. In other words, we will be careful not to quench the Spirit. When we really care about having God close, we will be more sin-conscious and more God-pleasing.

Dishonoring God's Presence

The next time you watch a movie or engage in a conversation, ask yourself, Is this honoring God? Will this invoke or quench His presence? Scripture warns us about quenching the Holy Spirit because it is first and foremost a sin, and all sin causes Him to grieve. Much to my chagrin, I have been guilty of quenching the Spirit. When I realize my wrong, I repent right away and ask God for His forgiveness. I really love God and don't want to cause Him to grieve. As a point of clarification, it is important for me to mention that when we grieve the Holy Spirit, He doesn't leave us. He remains omnipresent, but our sin causes Him to limit our access to His manifest presence. It's like God being in the general vicinity versus being up close and personal. If you want Him close to you, do what honors Him the most, which is to live to please Him.

Participating in the presence of God is also a part of our kingdom stewardship. This entails getting involved with what God is doing in our midst and helping to facilitate the process. Things such as resolving conflict in the workplace, solving money problems, or showing someone unconditional love are sound examples of how we can participate in God's presence. Christians are called to be facilitators of God's presence. We are responsible for creating environments where God can dwell. As ambassadors of Christ, our only motive must be to point people to Christ through our actions and decisions.

CHAPTER 6

The Principle of Oneness

ONENESS OR UNITY is the prevailing mandate of order in the kingdom of God. Oneness is the essence of the holy Trinity, comprised of three persons in one: the Father, the Son, and the Holy Spirit. Even though the Trinity is God in three persons, each with a distinct function, He is one God. Each person of the Trinity works together to support the entire entity with one unified purpose—to glorify God.

The triune God made all that was created. He created man to become one with Him, and as a result of this oneness, man would be fruitfully productive and God would be glorified in the heavens and the earth.

God specializes in bringing order to complete chaos. In Genesis 1:1–2, it is recorded that the Spirit of God hovered over the waters and brought order to a formless, chaotic earth: "In the beginning God created the heavens and the earth. Now the earth was formless and empty, darkness was over the surface of the deep, and the Spirit of God was hovering over the waters" (NIV). It is by the Spirit of God, the Holy Spirit, that order was created in the earth. It is by His gift of the same Spirit, through Jesus Christ, that order is to be maintained in the earth. God established His divine order to bring oneness (unity) to a broken and chaotic world. Order brings liberty. It is established, "Not by might, nor by power, but by my spirit, saith the LORD" (Zech. 4:6, KJV).

When we operate in unity, we bring God joy! The Bible says, "Fulfil ye my joy, that ye be likeminded, having the same love, being of one accord, of one mind" (Phil. 2:2, KJV). God commands oneness with Him in all of our doing and being. We are many members but one body. We have many functions but one purpose, which is to glorify God. There is one Christ, the Bridegroom, and one bride, the universal church.

Imagine the great works that could be performed if the body of Christ would dwell together in unity? Unity commands God's hand of blessing: "Behold, how good and how pleasant it is for brethren to dwell together in unity! It is like the precious ointment upon the head, that ran down upon the beard, even Aaron's beard: that went down to the skirts of his garments; As the dew of Hermon, and as the dew that descended upon the mountains of Zion: for there the Lord commanded the blessing, even life for evermore" (Ps. 133, KJV).

Unity is an equal-opportunity commodity, meaning it can be used for good or evil. In this world today we have witnessed horrific terrorist attacks and other acts of violence that killed thousands of men, women, and children. Somewhere along the line, there was unity among terrorists and other evildoers to carry out diabolical plans that resulted in the destruction of lives. I submit to you, if people can unite for evil and amass great destruction, surely the body of Christ can become one to do great exploits for the kingdom of God.

Protocol and the Trinity

Although equal in essence, the persons in the Trinity all have different functions. They execute their roles perfectly and perpetually. God the Father is Creator, God the Son is Savior, and God the Holy Spirit is our Helper.

Observe the protocol and divine order of the Trinity in the following scriptures:

> Jesus replied, "If I glorify myself, my glory means nothing. My Father, whom you claim as your God, is the one who glorifies me." (John 8:54, NIV). After Jesus said this, He looked toward heaven and prayed: "Father, the hour has come. Glorify your Son, that your Son may glorify you" (John 17:1, NIV). Jesus also said: "But when he, the Spirit of truth, comes, he will guide you into all the truth. He will not speak on His own; he will speak only what he hears, and he will tell you what is yet to come. He will glorify me because it is from me that he will receive what he will make known to you" (John 16:13–14, NIV). The Bible goes on to say, "For in him dwelleth all the fulness of the Godhead bodily" (Col. 2:9, KJV).

Let's look at Ephesians 1:11, "In Him also we have received an inheritance [a destiny—we were claimed by God as His own], having been predestined (chosen, appointed beforehand) according to the purpose of Him who works everything in agreement with the counsel and design of His will" (AMP).

Perfect Harmony

As you can see, the tri-functional, Godhead bodily operates according to divine order and has no other counsel but His own. God the Father's Counsel is comprised of three members of the Trinity in this order: (1) Father, (2) Son, and (3) Holy Spirit. The Godhead, although equal in essence, always acts and responds in divine order according to function. For example, look at the numbers one, two, and three. When it comes to the order of the Trinity, this authoritative headship functions in an ascending sequence (one, two, three), not in a descending sequence (three, two, one).

The attribution of Glory of the Trinity is demonstrated in the following fashion according to function: the Father (the 1st person of the Trinity) glorifies Jesus, His Son; Jesus (the 2nd person of the Trinity) glorifies the Father, and the Holy Spirit (the 3rd person of the Trinity) glorifies Jesus. The Trinity is three entities with corresponding functions, all comprising one God. Jesus said in John 10:30, "I and My Father are one" (NKJV). Jesus said in John 14:9, "Anyone who has seen me has seen the Father" (NLT).

As was demonstrated previously, God is the Father of divine protocol and order. He provided a divine relationship model by demonstrating and distinguishing the functionality of the varied roles of the Trinity. Nothing is moved, changed, enacted, or sanctioned without the agreement (oneness) of the Trinity, and with the Trinity, all things are possible. The Supreme Triune can never be defeated, never be impeded, and never be separated.

CHAPTER 7

Protocol of Worship

GOD CREATED WORSHIP for those who truly desire to know Him and love Him, for to know Him is to worship Him. John 4:24 says, "God is a Spirit: and they that worship him must worship him in spirit and in truth" (KJV). In worship there's a divine invitation, just like salvation, but only by choosing to worship Him will you be afforded the opportunity to receive a true revelation of who God is. God gives us a choice to worship because He said, "they that worship Him," not they must worship Him. And those who choose to worship Him must do so in "spirit and in truth" (KJV).

Just as you cannot really know a person until you share intimacy with them on some level, we cannot know God unless we worship Him. The good news is that salvation opens the door to intimacy with God, and worship is the threshold to intimacy with God. Worship is a byproduct of salvation. While it is true you must be saved by the grace of Christ Jesus, not every believer chooses to engage in worship. It's the same way in some marriages. Some couples are married in name only and don't engage in intimacy at all.

Although they are married, they lack the true intimacy God made available through the marital covenant. And let me be clear, the sex act alone does not equate to intimacy. Intimacy is the prelude, interlude, and postlude to sex. It's what you establish and maintain before you get to the bedroom and long after you leave the room. Sex without intimacy opens the door to an imposter. This is a flagrant violation, and it means intimacy has been forfeited or discarded.

No married couple is intimate with their clothes on. Those who choose to enjoy an intimate, sacred union do so in their nakedness. Naked in this sense means vulnerable, stripped, or exposed. This is the goal in true worship before the Father. He wants our whole being—spirit, soul, and body—without reservation. We belong to Him. When we give ourselves completely to God in worship, He transforms us into the image of Jesus (2 Cor. 3:18). So come, let us worship Him.

The Language of Love

Worship is also an invitation to intimacy with the Most High God. Jesus Christ is the gateway to worship and without Him no one can enter this realm. Worship is a place, the realm of truth, an existence, an eternal fire. Worship purifies. Worship is spiritual consummation with the Father of lights, and this union with the Father births the purest and fullest form of life. When you worship you will never be the same. You are forever changed and will always want to engage with Him. Worship demands the participation of the entire person. You will not tap into worship unless you are in a place of complete surrender.

Worship transcends time and blows the natural mind. Worship burns away the chaff of a stained, marred life. Worship removes the cloak of shame and replaces it with the garment of praise. Worship is a place where you're naked and never ashamed, and never the same. Worship is like a sterilized operating room filled with surgical tools and healing agents. It is the anesthesia that puts you under (your flesh) so that you can experience God's marvelous splendor (in spirit and in truth). Worship is like a romantic dance with our first love.

Come, ye naked, weary and broken to a place where your secrets can safely be spoken. In the secret place, we access the throne of heaven and eat of the bread of life. You can be made whole; you can be made clean, as the spotless and wrinkle-free bride being presented to her King.

In Sync With God

Worship is like a river advancing to a rhythm. The Spirit of God is the body of river moving to the syncopation of the life-giving Word that proceeds from the mouth of God. True worshippers join in with the river that is ever flowing. In this river there is love, faith, healing, peace, hope, deliverance, direction and more. True worshippers jump in as the water is troubled. It's time for Holy Communion; oneness with the Lover of our souls. United as one, we can move to the beat of the rhythm that love dictates. Love is the ever-flowing river that choreographs all movement, and we must wait in anticipation and respond in syncopation with the dictates of the Spirit. This rhythmic dance is uninterrupted because it is eternal—there is no beginning and no ending.

Here are some rhythmic, worship-filled scriptures:

- There is a river whose streams make glad the city of God, the holy habitation of the Most High. —PSALM 46:4, ESV

- Let them praise His name with dancing; let them sing praises to Him with timbrel and lyre. —PSALM 149:3, NASB

- Praise Him with timbrel and dancing; praise Him with stringed instruments and pipe. —PSALM 150:4, NASB

- And it shall come to pass, that every thing that liveth, which moveth, whithersoever the rivers shall come, shall live: and there shall be a very great multitude of fish, because these waters shall come thither: for they shall be healed; and every thing shall live whither the river cometh. —EZEKIEL 47:9, KJV

- Then the angel showed me the river of the water of life, bright as crystal, flowing from the throne of God and of the Lamb. —REVELATION 22:1, ESV

When believers worship, the portals of the heavens open, in response to our worship. The Father invites us to dance with Him. And the good news is, we don't have to wait until we get to heaven to dance. We can dance now! We can dance forever! Worship is now; it's right here and over there; worship can be found everywhere. True worshippers are truth worshippers. The Bible says, "But the hour cometh, and now is, when the true worshippers shall worship the Father in spirit and in truth: for the Father seeketh such to worship him" (John 4:23, KJV).

Those are the words Jesus spoke to the Samaritan woman at the well. Earlier in John 4, Jesus told the woman what happens when "whosoever" drinks the water He gives. Jesus said they "shall never thirst; but the water that I shall give him shall be in him a well of water springing up into everlasting life" (John 4:14, KJV). After the Samaritan woman's encounter with Jesus, she went on to tell others in John 4:29, "Come, see a man, which told me all things that ever I did: is not this the Christ?" (KJV).

Well, if that isn't a worship experience, I don't know what is! Jesus is still extending the invitation to worship today. Are you thirsty for the living water, Jesus? Then come and drink of this water and never thirst again. It's time to worship.

Obedience Is Not Optional

Jesus said, "If you love me keep my commandments" (John 14:15, KJV). To love Him is to obey Him, but the obedient lifestyle can only be achieved by surrendering to the power of the Holy Spirit and meditating on and walking in God's Word daily. When we submit our natural desires to God's supernatural power, it is a pure act of obedience. Jesus knew that mere mortals did not have the natural ability to keep His commandments. Think about this—it is not natural to obey a supernatural command, such as love your enemies. Say what? Or "bear with each other and forgive one another if any of you has a grievance against someone. Forgive as the Lord forgave you" (Col. 3:13, NIV).

How can we forgive or sin less without the aid of the Holy Spirit? We cannot forgive or be cleansed of any sin in and of ourselves. This is why God sent Jesus. Jesus is the propitiation for our sins, which means God was only satisfied when Jesus took on the sins of the world through His death on the cross and His victorious resurrection. And when Jesus ascended to the Father, He sent the Comforter, the Holy Spirit, to enable us to live for and serve God. Through the enabling power of the Holy Spirit, believers possess the ability to obey God sacrificially. Obedience requires faith, and implicit in a believer's faith is always sacrifice.

> Matthew 16:24–26 says: "Then Jesus told his disciples, 'If anyone would come after me, let him deny himself and take up his cross and follow me. For whoever would save his life will lose it, but whoever loses his life for my sake will find it. For what will it profit a man if he gains the whole world and forfeits his soul? Or what shall a man give in return for his soul?'" (ESV).

Denying self is a daily sacrifice, and anyone who does it for the sake of Christ lives his life in obedience to Christ. Obedience is the ordered lifestyle for every Christian.

Jesus said in John 15:5, "I am the vine, ye are the branches: He that abideth in me, and I in him, the same bringeth forth much fruit: for without me ye can do nothing" (KJV). We have been given the power to live a life that's pleasing to God. Hebrews 11:6 says, "And without faith it is impossible to please God, because anyone who comes to him must believe that he exists and that he rewards those who earnestly seek him" (NIV).

Without faith (active obedience) it is impossible to please God. He works in us through our obedience. But our disobedience blocks God's hand of blessing and ultimately leads us to defeat. This means our power becomes limited and our witness before others is hindered. The overarching fact of the matter is, when believers live a lifestyle that is not pleasing to God, the Holy Spirit is grieved. The Greek word *lypeo*, which is translated "grieve," means to make sorrowful or cause grief. Let us all be ever mindful of the damaging consequences of a disobedient lifestyle and, most importantly, how our disobedience grieves the Spirit of God.

God punishes disobedience because it is sin. Humans are not perfect, and God knows it. Sometimes we make bad decisions and mistakes, but when we obey God, we exercise our faith and invite God to act on our behalf. We cannot expect the rewards of obedience when we are disobedient. Disobedience is very costly. God will not contradict His Word; we must set ourselves in alignment with His Word.

Obedience is part of the law of sowing and reaping. Galatians 5:7 says, "Be not deceived; God is not mocked: for whatsoever a man soweth, that shall he also reap" (KJV). We know the difference between right and wrong. Whether we make right or wrong choices, we are sure to reap the consequences thereof.

There are many rewards for obedience. These include: knowing God's voice; intimacy with Christ; a victorious life; answered prayer; the salvation of our loved ones; a long, satisfying life; health; peace; success; protection; and wisdom. The benefits are endless. Although the immediate rewards of our obedience are not always evident, faith says we can always trust God for the outcome. The obedience you sow today will yield you an everlasting harvest tomorrow and on into eternity.

CHAPTER 8

A Warning About Witchcraft

MERRIAM-WEBSTER'S DICTIONARY defines rebellion as "open, armed, and usually unsuccessful defiance of or resistance to an established government." This definition reminds me of how Lucifer went from a beautiful, heavenly angel to the rebellious leader who led an unsuccessful revolt against God. (See Ezekiel 28.) He was defeated, of course, and was kicked out of heaven along with a third of the angels. But why would Lucifer give up his position with God? The answer is the same for anyone who exalts himself: pride.

Ezekiel 28:17 says, "Your heart became proud on account of your beauty, and you corrupted your wisdom because of your splendor" (NIV). His pride led him to openly defy the God who created him. Pride is the opposite of worship, it's self-exalting and self-consuming. Worship, on the other hand, causes the true worshipper to exalt God and surrender to Him.

When people operate in the spirit of witchcraft, they defy God. They usurp the rights, authority, and privileges of others for selfish pleasure or self-promotion. Acts 8:9–11 outlines a case of witchcraft: "But there was a certain man, called Simon, which beforetime in the same city used sorcery, and bewitched the people of Samaria, giving out that himself was some great one: To whom they all gave heed, from the least to the greatest, saying, This man is the great power of God. And to him they had regard, because that of long time he had bewitched them with sorceries" (KJV). Simon the sorcerer deceived many, but ultimately these same people became believers in Jesus Christ.

People who forfeit their personal power to others can become victims of witchcraft and will oftentimes fall prey to spiritual identity theft. This theft occurs when people lose a sense of who they are in Christ and start to seek their identity in another person or thing rather than God. This creates a void that cannot be legitimately filled by anyone other than God. Only He can identify and fully satisfy the desires of His beloved creation.

Jesus sent the Holy Spirit on the day of Pentecost to dwell in the heart of every believer. Christ gave His bride a Helper to empower her to live righteously and obediently. This is the Holy Spirit's assignment, but what does witchcraft have to do with order and protocol? The Holy Spirit is our Teacher, and it is imperative that man not exercise an independent mindset, which is a form of rebellion, when it comes to stewarding the things of God. Again, it is the Holy Spirit's job to empower us to be good stewards for God. It means that our loved ones, our jobs, our relationships, and the assignments God has given us to fulfill must be surrendered to the Spirit. He is the Conductor, and we must die daily to ourselves and to our selfish desires. Lord, help us.

It is recorded in Psalm 24:1: "The earth is the Lord's, and the fullness thereof; the world, and they that dwell therein" (KJV). Let me make it clear: everything belongs to God. He put all things on this earth on loan to man, not to be "owned" by man. Man's job is to steward what God has given him under the unction and function of the Holy Spirit. But whenever man refuses to submit to the leading of the Holy Spirit, he is disobedient. And disobedience always opens the door to demonic influence, thereby giving the enemy a foothold and legal access to carry out his wicked schemes.

We must avoid the traps of witchcraft, but we cannot do it without God's help. Scripture reminds us to always be on guard against the enemy. First Peter 5:8 says, "Be sober, be vigilant; because your adversary the devil, as a roaring lion, walketh about, seeking whom he may devour" (KJV). We must submit ourselves to God, resist the devil and he will flee (James 4:7). Adam and Eve were influenced by Satan to sin against God by eating from the tree of the knowledge of good and evil (Gen. 3). Even though Eve was the first to disobey God by eating the forbidden fruit, the couple didn't lose their God-given dominion and authority until Adam disobeyed God in the same way. Because God placed Adam (man) over Eve (woman) as the earthly authority figure, God made him accountable for her (see First Corinthians 11:3). This explains why after Adam sinned, God went looking for him, not Eve. Adam and Eve became influenced by Satan and consequently were separated from God because of their disobedience. Christians who submit to a power other than the Most High God fall into the same trap.

A Roadblock to Worship

Satan has a plan. He would like nothing more than to see every human being spend eternity in the lake of fire with him. To do that he must gain control of the church and usurp her power and authority so the world will worship him. This loss of power occurs because of disobedience and ignorance, and this is all the permission Satan needs to permeate our space. He wants to control individuals and ultimately lure them outside the will of God and into his hands, which is exactly what he did to Adam and Eve. As the body of Christ, we must deny the devil access. We must not allow him to embody or influence our space. Be ever mindful that when we disobey God, or when we are ignorant of the enemy's devices, we lose our spiritual footing. We lose territory and consequently forfeit our God-given dominion and authority.

Wherever there is a void or an empty space, it will either be filled by the Holy Spirit or by the demonic. When God inhabits an empty space by His Spirit, it becomes a place of worship. If the demonic enters, it will be a place of witchcraft, control, and oppression.

As Christians, God demands all our heart, spirit, soul, and body. This is worship in its purest form. We must war constantly to yield every member of our being to God. This is worship in warfare form. Any area of our lives that is not yielded to God is an open door to witchcraft. Our members are constantly at war with one another, oftentimes like members in the church. There is constant warfare—a battle—for our worship, our attention, and our allegiance. As believers, we must war over our worship to make sure it is not perverted or converted to witchcraft. We must protect that which only belongs to God.

Praise and worship go hand-in-hand. The Hebrew word, *halal* is a word for *praise*. This word simply means to shine; make a show, to boast, or rave about God, even to the point of appearing clamorously foolish. Anyone and anything can offer praise to God, even the stones! (See Luke 19:40.)

Now, think about these next statements in the context of worship. People seated in the general admission section of a public event, i.e., a pro football game, typically purchase the majority of the tickets sold but at a lower price. The seats in this section are the most affordable seats in the stadium but they are not necessarily the closest seats to the action on the field.

On the other hand, there are patrons who are willing to pay a higher premium to be seated in the VIP (Very Intimate Place) section just to be closer to the action on the field. The fact of the matter is, there is an open invitation for everyone to be seated in heavenly places in Christ Jesus but it's up to each individual to choose the seat he or she will occupy. When it comes to worshipping King Jesus, will we choose general admission seating or VIP seating? God has invited us all to move to the VIP section. The choice is ours.

Engaging in worship means we must strip off all our sins, cares, and troubles; get nakedly intimate with God; and implore Him to take over and SOS (save-oh-save) us! First Peter 5:7 says to "cast all your anxiety on him because he cares for you" (NIV).

Worship is God's divine invitation to become one with Him; to live and do life together. When we walk closely with God, we not only experience Him; we really begin to live for Him as He lives through us. To worship God means we covenant to walk with Him on this side of eternity until we get to worship Him eternally in heaven.

The Father designed the worship experience to be uninterrupted. Some Christians believe we can only experience this level of intimacy with God when we get to heaven, but I beg to differ. God's holy presence is with us here and now. Galatians 4:6 makes this clear: "And because ye are sons, God hath sent forth the Spirit of his Son into your hearts, crying, Abba, Father" (KJV).

When we worship Him, we enter the portals of heaven. Worship transports us from the temporal or earthly realm into the eternal realm, where God dwells. In fact, we have eternal life the moment we receive Jesus, according to John 17:3, "And this is eternal life, that they may know You, the only true God, and Jesus Christ whom You have sent" (KJV). The divine invitation remains open to anyone who accepts Jesus. I plead with you; do not miss having divine encounters with your heavenly Father while you are on earth.

Worship is also an opportunity to get God involved in your daily life, relationships, activities, and responsibilities. God desires to be included in every area of your life. Worship brings Him in the center of your experiences. When you don't keep yourself engaged in His presence, you won't experience the fullness of joy He provides.

Oftentimes as Christians we settle for intermittent and, at times, nonexistent God involvement and engagement in our lives. God is an equal opportunity God—He will allow you to commune with Him as much as you desire. Always remember, God invites you to encounter Him through worship, but whether you choose to worship Him is your decision.

As humans, we tend to want to be in control of things, people, and circumstances. We figure we can handle it all by ourselves—that is, until we get into trouble. But if we want God's best for our lives, we will have to be fully submitted to Him in every area of our lives. As Proverbs 3:5–6 says,

"Trust in the LORD with all thine heart; and lean not unto thine own understanding. In all thy ways acknowledge him, and he shall direct thy paths" (KJV).

CHAPTER 9

Initiating Relationships

IN ORDER FOR RELATIONSHIPS to function efficiently we must understand the purpose of relationships. God created man to be in fellowship (in relationship) with Him, not because He needed a relationship (He is the all-sufficient God) but because He had a plan. Note that Genesis 1:27 says, "So God created man in His own image, in the image of God he created him; male and female he created them" (ESV). God created man to be like Him to represent Him in the world, but the real work begins at home (homework).

Building and maintaining a relationship with God should be every Christian's single-minded pursuit. The more time we spend with Him, the more we become like Him. The more we know Him, the more we love Him. Everyone seeks to please the ones they love, but man's God-designed, sole purpose is to please Him, according to the apostle Paul. He wrote, "Whether, then, you eat or drink or whatever you do, do all to the glory of God" (1 Cor. 10:31, NASB).

Relationships are important to God for His plan of salvation and for building His kingdom here on the earth. When people accept Jesus Christ as their Lord and Savior, they enter a divine relationship. New converts to Christianity are given an opportunity to begin a love walk with the person of Jesus Christ through the Holy Spirit.

Whenever a relationship comes into play, agreement should be the ultimate goal. The Bible asks, "Can two walk together, except they be agreed?" (Amos 3:3, KJV). Whether for good or evil, relationships are synonymous with agreement. It's the only way any mission can be accomplished.

Recall the account in Genesis 11:1–9, where the people agreed to build what is known as the Tower of Babel to the heavens so they could make a name for themselves. When God saw this, He came down to confuse their language so the people would not understand one another. This created a clear division. God knew that because of the power of agreement, nothing would be impossible for them if they kept working together.

When it comes to building relationships, not only is agreement important but also remember that relationships should be reciprocal and not one-sided. While it is more blessed to give than to receive, don't give just to receive. When God joins people in relationships, it is never meant to be one-sided. God-designed relationships are to be mutually beneficial and for iron to sharpen iron.

We Must Practice the Golden Rule

Many have heard it said, "Treat others the way you want to be treated." This is so important to God. The Scripture says, "Do to others as you would have them do to you" (Luke 6:31, NIV). Too often we make the mistake of becoming so familiar with those closest to us that we end up treating them worse than anyone. We treat those we love most in a way we wouldn't dare treat people outside of our inner circle. Why? Because we are comfortable.

Perhaps we have taken our loved ones for granted by assuming they will always be around. Just because we are related to someone, or have been friends for a long time, doesn't mean that person will always stick around. Even the best of friends separate sometimes. People leave, people move, people die, and people sometimes lose interest or become incompatible. We must learn to value and nurture our relationships, especially those closest to us, so that those relationships are not jeopardized or lost prematurely.

No matter the type of relationship, it is important to know who belongs in your life and what role that person should play. Not everyone fits, and when it comes to relationships, one size does not fit all. Because all of your relationships are not the same, the people in your life should not be granted equal access to your life. Put healthy boundaries in place. Some people can only handle knowing you on a casual level, such as a lunch buddy or acquaintance. Others may know more about you on a personal level but let me warn you: access should be granted according to the grace allotted for that relationship and not beyond. Seek God for the grace, and He will help you set the proper boundaries.

There is a specific purpose for all relationships. Some are ordained by God while others are the work of the enemy.

We need God's wisdom to know the difference because God is the revealer of all hearts, and only He can turn hearts, good or evil, to benefit His purposes and plans.

Recall, if you will, Jonathan's devotion to David in 1 Samuel 23: "And Jonathan, Saul's son, arose and went to David at Horesh, and encouraged him in God. Thus he said to him, 'Do not be afraid, because the hand of Saul my father will not find you, and you will be king over Israel and I will be next to you; and Saul my father knows that also'" (vv. 16–17, NASB). This relationship clearly served God's purposes. Jonathan's allegiance to David was a pivotal factor in helping David become Saul's replacement as king. Saul wanted to kill David, but God used Saul's son, Jonathan to protect David. Jonathan was a friend in the right place and at the right time in David's life.

Give God your heart, and He will open your eyes to His truth. Always seek the Father for wisdom in all of your relationships because the health of your soul depends on it. Life or death is in our relationship choices. We must clearly discern and respect the differences in the roles people play in our lives, because as I stated previously, every relationship has a unique, distinct purpose. Some relationships include people you can safely reveal your heart's desire to, such as a family-like friend, sister, brother, or people who share your life's philosophy. Bear in mind, no one person fits this entire bill. It is not wise or healthy to expect to fulfill all your relational requirements from one relationship. To do so is unfair and self-defeating.

Learn to love and appreciate the people God has placed in your life but do this because of the uniqueness each person brings to your life. Every relationship has a unique purpose, and any unrealistic expectations outside of that purpose will lead to severe disappointment and hurt.

A Biblical Model of Friendship

In Exodus 25, God told Moses to tell the people to make Him a sanctuary so He could dwell among them. God provided all the specs and components for this sanctuary, which is also known as the tabernacle. As it relates to this model, there are three constructs I want to mirror in terms of relationships: the outer court, the inner court, and the tabernacle, which had two components, the holy place and the holy of holies.

Similarly, I submit to you that there are three types of friends. Some friends need to be acquaintances only, which represents the outer court. For example, there may be something about you or the other person that you engage with in a casual, public, or cursory setting. This is a non-intimate relationship with limited, infrequent engagement. You could have multiple acquaintances.

Another type of friend represents the inner court. There are fewer people in this type of friendship because these are more than acquaintances; these are the individuals you might hang out with on occasion. And since you don't hang out with everyone you meet, the numbers would be smaller in the inner court friendship than in the outer court acquaintances. The inner court friend is the one with whom you would have dinner or lunch; you would go shopping with this person and invite him or her to your house. This is a casual friend with whom you may share common interests, hobbies, likes, and dislikes.

There is another classification of friendship I will reference as the holy of holies. Perhaps you have heard it said that people enter our lives for a reason, a season, or a lifetime. Well, the friendships on the "holy of holies" level are typically the kind that last a lifetime. These are the "'do or die" friends and family members. They are there for you, and you are there for them no matter what. These friends know some of your deepest dreams, secrets, and desires.

When we cross or confuse the boundaries of the various types of friendships, hurt, abuse, and betrayal are inevitable. Sharing the right information with the wrong person can leave you vulnerable and wounded. It is very much like handing the sheep over to the wolves, or casting pearls before swine. Don't do it. If you have crossed these boundary lines, as many of us have, draw some new ones right away. As we learn to steward our relationships, let's keep these scriptures in mind:

> A man who has friends must himself be friendly, but there is a friend who sticks closer than a brother.
>
> —PROVERBS 18:24, NKJV

> As we have therefore opportunity, let us do good unto all men, especially unto them who are of the household of faith.
>
> —GALATIANS 6:10, KJV

When building and fortifying a friendship, it is important to recognize the type of relationship it is, what stage the relationship is in, and when there's a shift in the relationship. Friendships can be ruined by not understanding the purpose for which they were formed. If we are not careful, we may find ourselves trying to make an acquaintance our best friend when they were only meant to be an acquaintance. Bringing the wrong person in close and keeping the right person on the outskirts can prove to be tragic.

Establishing and maintaining relationships truly requires unconditional love, forgiveness, maturity, patience, prayer, and discernment. Here are some keys to preserving relationships:

- Watch your words. To quote my spiritual counselor, Dr. Rod Stodghill, "Learn to birth truth, don't just speak truth."
- Avoid judging others.
- Respect people's privacy and space.
- Be trustworthy and loyal.
- Create boundaries and honor other people's boundaries.
- Honor the roles and positions of others.
- Have real-ationships. Counterfeit relationships are a waste of time.
- Sensitize yourself to your environment. Discern what's happening around you.
- Learn to forgive yourself and others.
- Learn timing—know what to do, how to do it, and when to do it.
- Learn how to conduct yourself on a ministry assignment.
- Manage conflict appropriately.

This is certainly not an exhaustive list but it is a starting point. Relationships are important in life, and we must learn how to nurture them, work through them, and become better as a result of having experienced them. Every relationship encounter, whether good or bad, offers valuable lessons. Please discern the lessons so you can obtain the blessings.

Every relationship has a distinct purpose. Understand the purpose for each of your relationships, and then build your relationship around the specific purpose. Again, understanding purpose mitigates frustration and disappointment and puts things into perspective.

Cultivating Healthy Relationships

In every godly, healthy relationship an exchange takes place. Each person involved in the exchange comes away knowing and feeling something has been added to his or her life as a result of the exchange. If there are withdrawals during any phase of a relational transaction, and there will be, it is safe to assume that a deposit was previously made. In fact, deposits and withdrawals are made on a continual basis in order to establish and maintain a credit-friendly name. This presents a balanced relationship.

On the other hand, if relational transactions are not fluid, meaning if there's no rhythm of giving and receiving, the relationship can become unhealthy. Jesus said in Acts 20:35, "It is more blessed to give than to receive" (NASB). The text implies that receiving is still a blessing but giving is the greater blessing. The text also implies that giving and receiving go together; they are inseparable.

In unhealthy relationships you find *enablers* and *takers*, the antithesis of *givers*. *Enablers* habitually exceed the amount available in their account. They are overdrawn. They give until it hurts or hinders themselves and others. *Enablers* also incubate environments that attract *takers* by making repeated deposits hoping for a return. Both the *enabler* and the *taker* seek to selfishly reconcile their overdrafts, or voids, at the other's expense. These voids include the need for love, attention, acceptance, security, and affection. The *enabler* and the *taker* ultimately end up empty-handed. Not that anyone is keeping score, but it is wise to balance your relationship accounts to avoid overdrafts and service fees, which can be very costly. Only give out according to the grace you have been given. Deuteronomy 16:17 reminds us, "Each of you must bring a gift in proportion to the way the LORD your God has blessed you" (NIV).

The Spirit of God wants us to cultivate and preserve mutually beneficial relationships. Sometimes this involves having the tough, mature conversations in order to salvage relationships. If relationships are not working, they must be renegotiated or dissolved. Every relationship has its challenges, but if the tough conversations never happen, the relationships will ultimately corrode.

The fact of the matter is, sometimes relationships arrive at an impasse. The decision then becomes whether to move forward together or to separate. If the relationship moves forward, the impasse was an indication to take a new direction. If a separation occurs, focus on the lesson, not the loss. Focus on the value and not the cost.

Here are a few of my quotes on relationships:

"Relationships with two-sided equations mean both parties are doing the work. Even though each side brings different variables to the equation, they both bring balanced solutions to all types of problems."

"Healthy relationships, business or otherwise, must be mutually funded and mutually beneficial."

"It is important to separate friendships from business relationships. If a clear line is not drawn between the two entities, both relationships will be compromised and ultimately jeopardized."

"The currency of relationships is words and deeds."

CHAPTER 10

Protocol of Expectation

IN PSALM 62:5, the writer says, "My soul, wait thou only upon God; for my expectation is from him" (KJV). Any expectations outside of God will lead to disappointment. If we look to God as our Source, He will provide the resource. When we look outside of God and look to people as our source, we get off course and head for sure disappointment and frustration. My expectation is of the Lord.

God has given me various assignments throughout my journey with Him thus far. My most endearing assignments have been with ministries and families. Family has always been the most important component of my life, whether it was my immediate family, extended family or church family. Ever since I was a little girl, I have always had a deep love for family.

When my mother died in 2001 from kidney cancer, there was a huge void in my life. Within less than six months, my mother was diagnosed with cancer, had major surgery to remove her left kidney, underwent chemotherapy and went home to be with the Lord. Needless to say, I was devasted. Years prior to my mother's death, I never understood why God planted the following scripture in my heart: "God setteth the solitary in families: he bringeth out those which are bound with chains: but the rebellious dwell in a dry land" (Ps. 68:6, KJV). It was only after my mother's death that I began to experience God's faithfulness to me by setting me in a family.

My mother was my best friend and the glue that kept our family together. Although she and my father were divorced, throughout our childhood and adolescence my mother made sacrifices to care for and protect my two brothers and me, and continually provided the kind of love that emanated from God. It's because of God's love through her that I know what it is to love and be loved unconditionally. Imagine knowing this kind of love from a mother and then losing her too soon to death. It's very difficult to live without the mother's love you've known all your life. On a practical level, I know I never lost my mother's love, but the void of her physical presence created a longing in me to recoup what I thought I had lost. For a number of years I repeated a pattern of creating unrealistic expectations in relationships, all in a futile effort to fill the profuse void I had and still have today. I finally realized no one can ever replace the amazing relationship I had with my mother. Our relationship was a gift from God, and although my mother's physical presence is gone, her love will always remain.

After I submitted to God's call on my life, He sent me out of my comfort zone to serve both ministries and families over the course of eight years. When it came to the families I served, many times I got off track because I wanted to be *in* the families. God sending me to serve families meant moving in with the families. I recall my older brother warning me by saying, "Now Peri, you know how much you love family. But remember, it is important for you to maintain your own life and not become too involved in theirs." This was sound advice alright, but I did not follow it. After I moved in with one family, I became so enthralled with the family (like my brother said) that I lost my focus. I forgot about my plans and immersed my life right into the family. I lost myself! My expectation to become part of a family at this point was misguided and off track. I had to get back to the life I was responsible for living and creating. It was a hard road back, but I made it, thank God!

Unhealthy Expectations

An expectation is based on the principle of sowing. As a rule, we reap what we sow but we may not always reap where we sow. For instance, if we give a certain person our money, time, or lend a listening ear, it is reasonable to expect them to return the favor someday. The harsh reality is that person may never return the favor. Oftentimes, we set ourselves up for disappointment when we expect people to be there for us just because we were there for them. Sometimes that is not the case, but don't lose heart because God can use a different person to sow back into us.

Oftentimes we expect things from people that they cannot supply. We expect what we've given them, but people are different for a purpose. If I'm an apple tree, I produce apples. Oranges and apples come from trees, but an orange tree will never produce apples. The orange tree can only produce oranges. The orange tree is not a bad tree because it doesn't produce apples; it is a good tree specifically designed to produce only oranges. I cannot turn oranges into apples and nor should I try to. I must learn to appreciate the uniqueness of the orange tree. There are many trees in the forest, and each tree is unique. Study the tree for what it is, not what you want it to be. Appreciate and accept each unique creation and allow it to produce the purpose for which it was created.

I have made the mistake of trying to change others into what I wanted or needed them to be, only to be severely disappointed. It never worked, and it put undue pressure on the people I loved. The relationships also became strained and stressful. Expecting people to be and do what we desire is controlling behavior that sets us up for disappointment and heartache.

When I realized that I am the only person I can change, I began to work on changing myself. The changes I wanted to see in others were the changes that needed to take place in me. The things I expected from others were the very things I needed to wait on God to supply. God places people in our lives to help meet needs and solve problems, but He never created anyone to be who we want them to be, or to be the source and object of our desires.

God is the source for all our needs, and He uses people and other natural means as a resource to meet our needs. The great thing about having a need is God already knows what we need before we ask. God sees our need before we do, and He knows us better than we know ourselves. So whenever you have a need, seek God by using the familiar A.S.K. formula: ask, seek, and knock.

Ordered expectation is bringing our needs to God and allowing Him to supply those needs according to His plan, purpose, and timing, not ours. Scripture states it plainly in Philippians 4:19, "But my God shall supply all your need according to his riches in glory by Christ Jesus" (KJV).

CHAPTER 11

Protocol of Access

WHAT IS ACCESS? Merriam-Webster's dictionary offers this definition: "a way or means of entering or approaching." Many times we believers are given access to places that are not ours to manage—an amusement park, a department store, someone's home, or a church, for example. Let's look at a public place such as an amusement park, where the general public is granted paid access for a specified time.

The amusement park has the following protocols in place that address general admission requirements: the patron's age, weight, height, and health requirements for rides and proper behavior in the park. As long as the protocols are observed, access will be granted. But the moment any protocol is violated, any and all privileges can be immediately revoked, depending on the severity of the violation.

The protocols set forth in an environment are not designed to enslave but to ensure the safety of individuals and the profitability of the organization or business. Without guidelines to govern behavior, chaos will quickly ensue. Environments must be governed to establish and maintain order, efficiency, peace, prosperity, and security for all involved.

Protocols are the operating standard for every place or territory a Christian will be called to serve. Even Satan, an imitator and deceiver, must observe protocols. Satan knows the only way he can gain access to deceive or devour someone is when an individual is out of step or place with God. In fact, the Bible states in 1 Peter 5:8, "Be alert and of sober mind. Your enemy the devil prowls around like a roaring lion looking for someone to devour" (NIV). Evil can enter only when believers forfeit or are ignorant of their place. When Satan assumes an environment that is involuntarily or voluntary abdicated, he gains a foothold in the territory of the believer.

God created man in His image and likeness, and He gave him power to "rule over the fish of the sea and over the birds of the sky and over the cattle and over all the earth, and over every creeping thing that creeps on the earth" (Gen. 1:26, NASB). When we lose our footing or our place of authority, we give way to evil. Therefore, do not forfeit your access or territory. Do not get kicked out of the environment that was given to you by the blood and authority of Jesus Christ.

Access Is Your Power

It is critical for members of the body of Christ to observe and obey the protocols set forth in any environment where they have been granted access. This ensures victory! How do we know what the protocol is for an environment? The first thing to do is be led by the Holy Spirit. "But the Advocate, the Holy Spirit, whom the Father will send in my name, will teach you all things and will remind you of everything I have said to you" (John 14:26, NIV). The Holy Spirit is your Helper and your Teacher. He will teach you "the way" (direction and behavior) you should go.

Access can also be granted because of money, prestige, who you know, who knows you, or favor. If you are given access by the means of favor, that means someone likes you, and/or God has deemed you trustworthy in a certain area. Keep in mind, access gets you in the door, but your behavior and character determine how long you stay. I've heard many say, "Favor ain't fair." I once heard renowned pastor and best-selling author Bishop T.D. Jakes say, "Your gift can take you where your character can't keep you."

Do you qualify for the realm of access? Can you keep secrets, or are you a betrayer? The answers to those questions will determine whether you can be trusted. The higher you go, the more you will see and be exposed to. And depending on how well you manage what you see, you may see even more on a greater level. If you see little and mismanage the little, even that will be taken from you. It's all about stewardship. Can you handle what God has given you? The last thing we want to see is "access denied"! No one wants to hear Jesus say, "I never knew you: depart from me, ye that work iniquity" (Matt. 7:23, KJV). The following scripture details what happens to individuals who mismanage what they have been given (bad stewards): "So take the talent from him and give it to him who has the ten talents. For to everyone who has will more be given, and he will have an abundance. But from the one who has not, even what he has will be taken away" (Matt. 25:28–29, ESV).

Because we are merely stewards, we must keep in mind that what we have been given in this life is not ours; it all belongs to God. And how well we manage a thing (gift, talent, or relationship) will determine how long we steward it. It is a grave mistake to think that just because we have managed a thing, we have a right to own it or will always have access to it. That's entitlement, which is an ownership mentality. As stewards, we are not entitled to anything in God's kingdom. We don't own it; we've been loaned it—and only by the grace and lordship of Jesus Christ.

When it comes to stewardship, allow me to issue a warning about assumptions. Just because you have keys to unlock a building doesn't mean you've been granted full access to every room in that building. Each key on the key ring has a specific assignment. And although you have access to the whole building, do not assume you can unlock a door and enter a room where you have not been invited. Be clear about the expectations of your assignment and abide by the instructions therein. Refrain from entering places where you haven't been invited or have been denied access.

God gave Adam and Eve full access to the Garden of Eden; however, He gave them specific instructions about where to make their food selections. He said they could eat freely from any tree of the garden. But from the tree of the knowledge of good and evil they could not eat, and if they did they would surely die (Gen. 2:16–17). But when Adam and Eve decided to disobey God and eat of the forbidden tree, He booted them out of the garden. Think about this. Adam and Eve's one wrong choice has impacted mankind for centuries.

There is a governed behavior for each room you enter. Be mindful that your misconduct in any one room can cause you to be denied access to all rooms. Your access to more is in how you handle the first door. Observing and honoring protocol is the key to entering the next door, and each door has a specific protocol. You will be given a key. You will be offered a door. Manage the key and door God has offered you and don't try to access the ones you desire but haven't been given access to.

There is some access you've been given that you need to relinquish because it's either time, it wasn't yours to have, or it was not yours to keep. Yes, sometimes you must hand over the keys you've been given, because even though the key still unlocks the door, the door is no longer suitable for you.

Sometimes you've been given access to things and people that hold you hostage. Don't use the very key you've been given to imprison yourself. Don't lock yourself into a person or system that no longer suits you, or to a system that is designed to imprison you. Throw away the key and be free.

Jesus Is the Only Way

There are three levels of access to the door of salvation. Let's look at the example of the Trinity: Father, Son, and Holy Spirit. How do you get to the Father? There is one way, "the Door," who is Jesus! How do you experience Jesus? By repenting of your sins and accepting Christ in your heart as your Lord and Savior. How do you access the Holy Spirit? By way of Jesus. Any way we approach it, the Word says we must enter first through Jesus: "Jesus answered, 'I am the way and the truth and the life. No one comes to the Father except through me'" (John 14:6, NIV). We must prove to be trustworthy in the outer courts in order to experience the inner courts of God's glory!

The Book of Esther is a great example of how protocol was used to both lose and gain access to a king. In this story, the king of Persia ousted his queen, Vashti, because she disobeyed his command to come before him. Vashti literally embarrassed the king in front of his guests. In a marriage, there are some things couples can do behind closed doors, but when a private move is made in public, it can cost them the kingdom. Vashti paid a great price for embarrassing her king.

Esther, on the other hand, pleased the king and found favor in his sight. She had been schooled in the art of kingdom protocol by her Uncle Mordecai, who taught her how to gain access and obtain the keys to the kingdom, not just for herself but for a whole nation of Jews.

Vashti took a gamble by disobeying her husband the king, and she lost her kingdom privileges. Esther took a gamble by trumping protocol, and the king used it to win a nation. What's the difference? Vashti was disobedient and selfish while Esther was obedient and selfless. Esther even went so far as to say, "And if I perish, I perish" (Est. 4:16, ESV). She knew she was putting her life on the line when she made her appeal to the king. This was a deviation that could have meant Esther's annihilation and all the Jews, but instead God used it to grant access to freedom for all.

CHAPTER 12

Protocol of God's Glory

IN ORDER TO STEWARD God's glory in the earth we must first understand what this word means. One of the Hebrew words translated *glory* is *kabad*, which can mean "'honor,' 'great,' or 'weighty.'"

Can you handle the weight of the glory—God's glory, that is? God's goodness is the manifested essence of His presence. God has entrusted His glory to the church because He desires to sit down, show off, and rest His glory upon us. We cannot steward or manage God's glory; we can only give glory to whom all the glory is due! We can only return to Him the attribution of His goodness. God decides where His glory will be on display, not the "glory carrier," the body of Christ.

When God is pleased, honored, and glorified, He shines the glory on the object of His pleasure. Man has his own glory, and it emanates from man. The glory of man is temporal and fades away, moment by moment. Man's glory perishes, but God's glory is everlasting. Though the outward man perishes, the inward man is being renewed day by day (2 Cor. 4:16). The glory of God is heavy, weighty. God chooses and prepares the vessel to display His glory. The preparation comes through much trial; the heavier the glory, the greater the trial. The glory will put pressure on your life so you will come out of the trial like pure gold. You will have to go through the fire to see the glory. Through the trial you will be tried by fire until it produces the pure gold of God's glory.

The only way to receive the glory is through the fire. That means there will be tests. Just as a man does not steward the glory of God, neither can he choose the test God will use to try him. God will test you. I am a living witness. I have gone through some fires I didn't think I would come out of, but when I did, others witnessed the glory of God on my life. The great news about undergoing the fire of God's glory is that He is right there in the fire with you. In fact, He has gone before you to show you the end, which is your victory through Christ.

In Daniel 3, God displayed His glory when the three Hebrew boys were bound and thrown in the fiery furnace. The fire was turned up seven times hotter than the usual temperature, but they were not consumed. In fact, Scripture records that they walked around in the fire with a fourth man, who we know to be Jesus. God demonstrated in this example that the hotter the fire, the greater the glory! We can have the same testimony as the three Hebrew boys: "But he knows where I am going. And when he tests me, I will come out as pure as gold" (Job 23:10, NLT). The fire of God's glory is meted out only by Him. He knows how much of His fire we can take. Simply put, the vessel does not come forth from the fire until the Master is pleased. Sometimes you may have to holler, cry, or kick, but you will not be consumed. Hold on to the truth of this scripture: "When thou passest through the waters, I will be with thee; and through the rivers, they shall not overflow thee: when thou walkest through the fire, thou shalt not be burned; neither shall the flame kindle upon thee" (Isa. 43:2, KJV).

God's glory is so hot that if anyone touches it, he can be burned or even consumed. We cannot own what only belongs to God. His glory is His alone. The glory can touch us, but we can't touch the glory.

Value Your Gifts

We must know the inestimable value of our gifts, which come from God. Christians—that is, those who have accepted Jesus Christ as Lord and Savior and have been washed in His blood—have been given gifts from the Lord. And, as it is written, to whom much is given, much is required. Yes, all Christians are responsible for managing and appropriating their gifts. It is the Christian's duty to count the cost and help save the lost. How do we do that? Through the various gifts the Lord has graced us with through the power of the Holy Spirit.

Every member of the body of Christ must know and be familiar with how the Holy Spirit has graced them. We can place no value on what is unknown until the unknown becomes known. We must know our value. We must know our *power lanes* and get in them if we want to perform great exploits for the kingdom.

Whether we have the gifts of healing, teaching, faith, or edification, we are responsible for how those gifts are used, and we will be judged by God based on how we administrate our gifts. Simply put, all Christians will be held accountable for how we have administered our gifts. What do I mean? For example, did you pray about when and where to use the gifts you were given? Did you perfect the gift? Did you pimp the gift or allow others to pimp the gift? Did you share the gift or use it for your personal gain? Were you too afraid to share your gift? Did you feel your gift wasn't good enough? There is no room for excuses! We will all have to give an account for the gifts God has given us.

Do you know the cost of the anointing on your life? The cost is spelled out in Romans 12:1, "Therefore I urge you, brethren, by the mercies of God, to present your bodies a living and holy sacrifice, acceptable to God, which is your spiritual service of worship" (NASB). God will not accept anything less. Following God's call on your life will cause you to die to your own desires and plans. The call could cost you relationships, jobs, and even separation from the people you love most. The cost is your cross. Matthew 16:24–25 says: Then Jesus said to His disciples, 'If anyone wishes to come after Me, he must deny himself, and take up his cross and follow Me. For whoever wishes to save his life will lose it; but whoever loses his life for My sake will find it'" (NASB). There is a price you have to pay for serving and being used by God.

Have you counted the cost? Do you put a demand on what others are asking or expecting you to deliver? Do you discern the demands other people are placing on your gifts, or are you just happy that someone extended you an opportunity to put your gift on display? In other words, did you pray about it before you said yes?

Pray About Everything

I have been guilty of being so thrilled when people asked me to do something I love that I didn't stop to ask the Lord what

He thought of the idea. I just assumed it was Him and jumped in feet first only to realize sooner than later that God was not involved in my decision. Consequently, things did not pan out the way I had hoped. As a matter of fact, many times I gave away everything and came away with nothing. Something is wrong with that picture. When we pray about ministry opportunities, we still have to be prayerful, even when God gives us a yes. The work is not done; it's only begun.

Many years ago one of my spiritual mentors told me to do my homework on people I work with, particularly in ministry. This also includes my spiritual homework. Find out their track record, their reputation, and how they treat the people who serve them.

Obviously those looking to hire you in ministry have done their homework on you, because they are asking you to be a part of what they're doing. Well, let's not be so excited about opportunities that we don't seek God for direction. Many will come knocking, but we must always be prayerful and discerning because trouble will arise, especially when it's a God assignment. But there is no greater trouble than the trouble we encounter outside of God's will. The bottom line is, don't let people pimp you and don't pimp yourself. Second Corinthians 4:7 says, "But we have this treasure in jars of clay to show that this all-surpassing power is from God and not from us" (NIV). One must know how to qualify others and assess them based on whether they have the capacity to receive the gifts and the giver in a way that is honoring to the Lord. I have had some personal experiences where people knew the value of my gifts better than I did, but they had wrong motives. Conversely, I was ignorant about the value of my gifts but had pure motives. Neither case is a good scenario. This is why I assert that we as believers must know the value of our gifts in order to become better stewards.

If we properly steward our gifts based on knowledge, wisdom, and the leading of the Holy Spirit, we will make better choices about when, how, and with whom to share them. Mismanagement (bad stewardship) of gifts and talents in the body of Christ occurs when people do not value their gifts or the gifts of others. This can be due to ignorance or disobedience. Do not continue to fall prey to either. Educate yourself. There are spiritual gift assessments online that can help you discover your gifts.

If you become acquainted with the gifts God so freely gave you, you will begin to value your gifts and others' gifts. Ascribing value to a gift can mean showing honor, highlighting significance or worth through words, and even being paid money. Granted, all gifts do not have to come with a monetary price tag, but sometimes financial compensation is apropos, especially if you have spent time cultivating your gift and there's a great demand for it. The Bible states in 1 Timothy 5:18, "'You shall not muzzle the ox while he is threshing,' and 'The laborer is worthy of his wages'" (NASB). If you work, you must be paid. If you hire someone for a service, the godly thing to do would be to pay the person for that service.

The late Myles Munroe said, "If you don't know the purpose of a thing, abuse is inevitable." Matthew 7:6 addresses this issue: "Do not give what is holy to the dogs; nor cast your pearls before swine, lest they trample them under their feet, and turn and tear you in pieces" (NKJV).

The overall lesson is to cultivate and use your gifts wisely because one day you will have to give an account of your deeds to Jesus! The Owner (Jesus) is coming back to collect what belongs to Him.

You Have the Power to Change

Every environment has an established order, and when God created the earth He called it to order, thereby making it habitable for every living creature He put on the earth. In Genesis chapter 1 we see God's architectural handiwork. God was so detailed in His design that He prepared and innately equipped all earthly inhabitants with everything they would need to thrive in their specific habitat. The fish were created for the sea, the fowl for the air, and mankind and other creeping things for the land.

Environments were designed to be enjoyed, accommodating, and habitable. With that in mind, environments were also made to be conducive to their inhabitants. Inhabitants of a land or territory include animals, insects, rodents, mammals, and Homo sapiens (human beings). Typically, inhabitants that are indigenous to a certain region or climate are well-suited and innately equipped to thrive in their environments. But even so, the weather can change, causing climatic shifts in an environment and the inhabitants will have to either adjust or leave altogether.

When it comes to people, they are going to either be subject to their environment or empowered to change their environment. To communicate it another way, people are either going to be a product of their environment or they are going to change what is produced in their environment.

The main point I want to make here is people have the power to change their environment, even if it means changing their location. If you don't like what your environment is producing—and by the way, your environment can even be you: your mind, will, and emotions—God has given us the power to change. Changing your mind means changing your life. Romans 12:2 says it best: "And do not be conformed to this world, but be transformed by the renewing of your mind, that you may prove what is that good and acceptable and perfect will of God" (NKJV).

Human inhabitants are not inclined to be somewhere they don't enjoy, nor do they wish to dwell in a place for which they are not well-suited. Who would? If you are in an environment you don't enjoy, your first inclination may be just to leave, but that may not always be the answer. Leaving is sometimes the easy way out, and it can be very costly. Perhaps you might consider how to improve your surroundings instead of just running away. After all, you could have been sent there by God to make a difference.

Finding God in Unusual Places

It was nearly seven years after my mother passed away that I began to fully obey God's call on my life in ministry. Soon after I showed up for duty, God sent me on various assignments that were totally out of my comfort zone. I was always very excited about heading out to the next assignment but was not at all excited about staying. In fact, there were many days I wanted to abort the mission altogether because oftentimes, as is life, things became unpleasant and uncomfortable. A few times I did just that; I left, only to find out later that I had to return because I was on a God assignment. I thank God that any place I left prematurely, He provided me with enough grace to return just before the door was permanently closed. Sometimes God will call you to unpleasant places and unpleasant experiences. These are situations and circumstances that are much beneath your preferred pleasure. The Lord's goal in all of this, however, is to change you (your mind) and prepare you to survive and thrive in any environment. He wants you to rule and rest in the environment, not run and reject the environment. Sometimes you will not like the skin you're in, but if it is God-fitted, you will not be acquitted. Do you get it?

There's an environment in every area of life. It could be the environment of culture. For instance, when a person uses profanity and it's not frowned upon, it's because profanity is acceptable in that environment. But sometimes a person is in an environment to change it. There's always someone in charge of an environment—the behavior in an environment is dictated and/or facilitated by the host of that environment. The host sets the tone of the environment, and others follow suit. Conversely, all environments are not suited for all people. In other words, some places may not be a good fit. How do you know? As a guest, it is wise to leave any environment that becomes hostile as a result of your presence. If the host does not defuse the situation, it is an indication that your presence is not welcomed. It's time to leave because the host of that environment dictates that environment, and whatever the host allows increases.

Always remember, your presence is a present. If your presence is not received as a gift to be enjoyed, it's time to be absent. Be willing to present, but whenever your presence is not received, properly count yourself absent. Based on what I've just discussed, I must conclude that there are two questions to ask yourself before entering an environment: Were you sent? Or did you just "went"? If you were sent, no matter the state of the environment, your presence there was for a purpose. I truly believe most environments can be salvaged and improved, just like some relationships. On the other hand, if I cannot improve or be improved by an environment, I must vacate the premises.

Consider how you may be contributing to the climate of your environment with your thoughts, words, and actions.

Don't assume everyone appreciates the environment you create, because not everyone will. Mark the people who do appreciate it, remember those who don't, and make the necessary adjustments. You decide who gets your time, so create the environment you desire wherever you are.

For Christians, the Holy Spirit is the heavenly host housed in the believer's spirit man. Therefore, Christians must be careful to create environments that honor God and others. We must protect and promote the glory of God's presence. If the environment is not conducive for God's presence, work to change it or make haste to leave it.

The Protocol of Presence

The word *presence* in this sense, refers to the present (gift) of a being, an idea, or concept; an impression; a suggestion; a belief; an action; or an influence. Presence can also include being in the company of someone else. Presence is meant to be shared and enjoyed. For instance, when someone decides to grace you with their presence (or vice versa) or to present you an offering of some kind, it should be a present. People don't have to be kind to you or share their time or resources with you. But when they choose to do so, it can impact your life in very positive ways.

However, presence does not always imply the company of another human being. God's presence can be company enough. This is why it's important to learn how to be "present" with God. No one knows you better than God, and when you allow yourself to be alone with Him you become one with Him and yourself. Aloneness is about oneness, and oneness is about being complete or whole. To communicate it another way, in order to be fully and authentically present, one must learn to be completely and comfortably alone with God. Being alone with the Father means being at home with

Him. This, my friends, is the ultimate gift of presence—learning to enjoy God's presence and your own.

It is very important for you to recognize that your presence is a present long before anyone else does. When you enjoy your company, you are very likely to be enjoyed in someone else's company. Just as you become at home with God's presence, be at home with your own presence. Be comfortable in your own skin.

Presence is also about presenting. What and to whom are you presenting? In order for your presence to be considered a present to others, it must first be of precious value to you. That way you will be able to decide what part of you to share with others. Be very selective, because everyone will not be worthy of the various levels of gifts your presence offers.

Think about what you offer other people when you are present. Keep in mind that your presentation should be representative of who you are but if you are not acquainted with yourself, your presence will be inauthentic. The real you is the God in you. When you give others your authentic presence, you give them the God in you. That's the part of you that glorifies Him; that's what God wants you to give to others and give back to Him. If you have not fully given yourself to God, you will invariably misrepresent Him in some form or another.

Pursuing God's Presence

Ideally, the ultimate presence we seek is God's, and if we endeavor to encounter His presence, it must be intentional on our part. As Christians, God's presence should be our preeminent and constant pursuit. We pursue what we're passionate about and what interests us. To put it another way, our pursuit dictates the route we take in life. Some pursue houses, relationships, and the like. What is your passionate pursuit? Once you know the answer, you can determine whether you need to continue your course or reroute your life. In Psalm 63:1–4 (KJV), David cries out to the Lord in his pursuit of Him:

> O God, thou art my God; early will I seek thee: my soul thirsteth for thee, my flesh longeth for thee in a dry and thirsty land, where no water is; to see thy power and thy glory, so as I have seen thee in the sanctuary. Because thy lovingkindness is better than life, my lips shall praise thee. Thus will I bless thee while I live: I will lift up my hands in thy name.

In Philippians 3:12–14 (NASB), Paul offers this example of what it looks like to pursue God with his life:

> Not that I have already obtained it or have already become perfect, but I press on so that I may lay hold of that for which also I was laid hold of by Christ Jesus. Brethren, I do not regard myself as having laid hold of it yet; but one thing I do: forgetting what lies behind and reaching forward to what lies ahead, I press on toward the goal for the prize of the upward call of God in Christ Jesus.

If you are jumping through hoops to pursue people who don't make an effort to spend time with you, I suggest you stop it. Think about what you're striving to do. More than likely, you have been spending time with people who don't celebrate you. If they knew how to celebrate you they would make a concerted effort to be in your presence. Never strive to be in people's presence if they don't make an effort to be in yours.

Keep in mind, the company you keep should be pleasant, like a sweet aroma. If people insult you and treat you with disrespect, they don't deserve to be in your presence. Recognize your worth. You are very valuable. It is better to be alone than to be around people who try to devalue you.

And don't devalue yourself. Learn to like and enjoy you! Self-respect will attract respect.

Be mindful that wherever you are present, God is present. Because He is alive in you, everywhere you show up, He's there. Christians belong to Christ, and wherever we go, He goes. When we enter environments that do not glorify Christ, the Holy Spirit always lets us know. For instance, if you enter a room where the conversation is negative or vile, you may feel grieved if you hang around too long. That would be an example of the type of atmosphere from which you need to make an exit. Because we are "glory carriers," we can no longer look at where "we" choose to go; we must discern and decide if that place will honor God's presence. As stewards of God's presence, we must constantly place His presence above our preferences.

Practicing Forgiveness

Forgiveness is not optional in the kingdom of God; it is a command. Scripture exhorts us to forgive in Mark 11:25, "And when you stand praying, if you hold anything against anyone, forgive them, so that your Father in heaven may forgive you your sins" (NIV). Notice that forgiveness is commanded of the one who holds the offense and not the offender. Also notice that the offended becomes the offender in this case, because God is offended when we don't forgive. Is it safe to say that the onus of forgiveness is on the person offended? My answer is yes, because even though God was offended by our offenses, He forgave us anyway. Romans 5:8 says, "But God demonstrates His own love toward us, in that while we were yet sinners, Christ died for us" (NASB).

The truth of the matter is the body of Christ cannot and will not function properly without regularly practicing the principle of forgiveness. Forgiveness is necessary for everyone, especially those who know Christ. Without forgiveness, there is no anointing, which means no power and no authority. One is simply rendered impotent without it. So what will it be? Will we choose to be empowered by God or be impotent by operating in our own strength?

To me, forgiveness means releasing a person from all wrongdoing; exonerating them from any harm they caused me or a loved one. Truly, this is easier said than done. To be honest, I sometimes wrestle with forgiveness, especially when I feel I've been wronged or hurt by someone. But when I realize I could hinder my relationship with the Lord by refusing to forgive, I immediately begin to release the person and let the offense go. One thing I've come to realize in life is that people will come and go, but God will always remain. I need God more than people, so I want to get this forgiveness thing right.

Forgiveness is not a one-time-only transaction. Forgiveness is a lifestyle, a way of living and loving. Let's look at the word *forgive* in reverse order. It reads "give for." Based on this example, I assert that forgiveness is a gift "given for" any and every offense known to man. We are without excuse. Forgiveness is by no means approving of someone's bad choices. Forgiveness is the decision to release a person and no longer hold him or her captive.

Why should we forgive? First, God commands us to forgive. Also, forgiveness is a gift to self. When we hold bitterness, anger, and resentment toward someone—even ourselves—we administer a form of death. It could be a form of death to our mental or physical health, or death to a relationship. When we truly forgive, life is released. That's why I say, "Forgive and live." And living is about giving and forgiving. Christ was the model of forgiveness. He forgave us of all our sins, including the ones we have yet to commit. Jesus forgave in advance. What a Savior He is!

How many times should we forgive others? "Then Peter came to Jesus and asked, 'Lord, how many times shall I forgive my brother or sister who sins against me? Up to seven times?' Jesus answered, 'I tell you, not seven times, but seventy-seven times'" (Matt. 18:21–22, NIV).

In this passage, Jesus is not limiting us to forgive others seventy-seven times. He simply provides the perfect model of forgiveness without limits. When we truly forgive others, we should lose count of how many times we forgive them. And when we lose count, we ultimately stop counting altogether and just forgive.

Christian writer and teacher R.T. Kendall wrote the following in his book *Total Forgiveness*:

"Detached forgiveness—there is a reduction in negative feelings toward the offender, but no reconciliation takes place.

Limited forgiveness—there is a reduction in negative feelings toward the offender, and the relationship is partially restored, though there is a decrease in the emotional intensity of the relationship.

Full forgiveness—there is a total cessation of negative feelings toward the offender, and the relationship is fully restored."

Forgiveness is both a gift to self and a gift to others. We are commanded to forgive abundantly because in our mortal bodies we are all prone to sin and offending others. By forgiving others (and in many cases ourselves) we demonstrate the love of Christ, which is shed abroad in our hearts.

The more we love, the more we can forgive. The more we forgive, the more we love. When God speaks to you about forgiveness, He's concerned about your heart and not how or if others will receive your forgiveness. Forgive and live! Forgiveness is hard, but unforgiveness is harder (on you).

CHAPTER 13

Protocol of Divine Assignment

DIVINE ASSIGNMENTS ARE "assigned" by God. When you answer God's call to service, you must be open to His direction. His direction will lead you to His assignment(s) for your life.

What is an assignment? An assignment is the kingdom "homework" you are required to complete. Your "home," which will vary, will be the place where you are required to "work" to complete all course requirements in an exemplary fashion. Throughout the course of your life assignment(s), you may be called to a person or people, work or duty, or to a specific place or region for kingdom purposes. Essentially, your assignments are your *marching orders* from the chief commander and CEO of the universe, our heavenly Father.

God has chosen you for a specific assignment or various assignments throughout your lifetime, and if you haven't a clue about where you belong, the obvious answer is to seek

Him. God knows the purpose for which He made you. It's time for you to know the why of your existence and pursue it with persistence.

Allow me to reiterate, you do not choose your assignment; God does. Who we are and hope to become are found only in Him. The church is the body of Christ. When we are truly in His service we become His mouthpiece, arms, legs, feet, ears, eyes, etc. "What? know ye not that your body is the temple of the Holy Ghost which is in you, which ye have of God, and ye are not your own? For ye are bought with a price: therefore glorify God in your body, and in your spirit, which are God's." (1 Cor. 6: 19-20, KJV). Members of the body of Christ belong to God, and that means we are owned by Him.

There's no need to worry if we can be successful, because God has anointed the body of Christ to carry out tasks with strategy, efficiency, precision and excellence to achieve explosive results. Many understandably become excited about carrying out specific tasks for the Lord. That's a good thing but it's also a prepared thing, because whenever there is a divine calling, there's always divine preparation. God knows how to strategically prepare and equip us for where we're going. Therefore, you will undergo a series of tests and trials; you will encounter the right (and wrong) people and conflicts; and you will overcome any and all obstacles through your obedience and by His power. You must endure this preparation process despite the many pitfalls you will encounter.

Know Your Assignment

Most often your current assignment is preparation for your next assignment. Yes, the lessons, tests, and trials will continue. And if you refuse the lessons from the present assignment, you will inevitably repeat the coursework, because God loves you too much to allow you to fail. God wants to trust us with more. We don't have to earn His love, but we do have to earn His trust.

God desires to expand your borders by developing your competence and character in your assignments. You will be stretched, you will be inconvenienced, and you will even want to run the other way but stay the course. I always say, "Get the lesson so you can get the blessing," and, "Favor gets you in the door, but your attitude and aptitude determine your overall score." Always remember, assignments are not arrival points; they are your journey points. I had to learn this.

Be obedient in your assignment, and God will reward you. Be obedient in your assignment even when others are disobedient. Perform when others refuse to. God grades us on our individual merit, not on our neighbor's merit. When I was a child, I got in trouble with my parents whenever I told them, "So-and-so's parents let them do such and such, why can't I?" My parents did not like that question at all because their focus was on me growing and learning. My scholastic report cards assessed my performance in my studies, not someone else's. Your score is not contingent on other people's behavior; it's based solely on your behavior. Someone else's disobedience does not cancel out your obedience. Remember, God always rewards obedience.

Excellent Gifts

In the body of Christ, there are many gifts but the same Spirit, and there are many members but one body. First Corinthians 12 outlines the spiritual gifts apportioned to the body of Christ by the grace of God through the Holy Spirit, the giver of all good gifts and perfect gifts.

All gifts in the body of Christ were designed by God to be given: "Freely you have received; freely give" (Matt. 10:8, NIV). This command from God is proof that giving and receiving go hand in hand. Any gift offering that is void of either giving or receiving is an incomplete offering. Gifts that are given and received benefit the entire body. "For God so loved the world that he gave his one and only Son, that whoever believes in him shall not perish but have eternal life" (John 3:16, NIV). The best gift, which is Jesus Christ, was given by the Father and has been received by many. He truly is the most excellent gift.

When it comes to the gifts in the body of Christ, there is no room for selfishness, pride, or arrogance. Anytime we take on those attitudes, it means we have developed a selfish mindset, whereby we consider ourselves owners instead of stewards. We think we have a right to control or manipulate the gifts we have been given. For instance, if we feel afraid to use our gifts, we hold them back. If we feel unworthy of our gifts, we suffocate them or promote someone we think is better than we are at utilizing that gift. The gift-bearer is also responsible for cultivating, sharpening, and exercising his or her gifts and sharing them with others. The Bible clearly says to whom much is given, much is required (Luke 12:48).

The Power of Servanthood

We rarely hear sermons today about how to be a servant of Jesus. Christ, however, was the personification of servanthood here on the earth, and we are called to follow in His footsteps. Servanthood doesn't come natural to humans, but Jesus gives us a biblical example in Matthew 18: 1–4 of what it looks like: "At that time the disciples came to Jesus and asked, 'Who, then, is the greatest in the kingdom of heaven?' He called a little child to him, and placed the child among them. And he said: 'Truly I tell you, unless you change and become like little children, you will never enter the kingdom of heaven. Therefore, whoever takes the lowly position of this child is the greatest in the kingdom of heaven'" (Matt. 18: 1–4, NIV).

Jesus demonstrated the servant model in His service to mankind and to His disciples. He taught us that servanthood is love, obedience, and sacrifice. Jesus also taught us that in order to be great we must become a servant to mankind. Jesus is the perfect Servant King.

When you are truly a servant, you can serve anyone as the Lord leads. True servants don't just serve the popular, celebrities, or people they like. A true servant always has a heart for service, no matter who is present. A true servant seeks to serve a need.

Sometimes servants are mistreated by people who don't have a proper understanding of servanthood. Frankly put, some people view servants as slaves. Let me encourage you to remain a servant even when others treat you like a slave. Even when they treat you like a king, remain a servant because a servant is a king!

Always know who you are before you serve, remember who you are while you are serving, and know that God's greatest desire for you is to remain His servant. Whether you're serving in ministry or on a job, it is important that you keep in mind the following two things: (1) God sent you on assignment as His representative, and (2) whenever you serve others, you serve God. As long as you keep these things in mind, you won't get confused about who you are and what you were sent to accomplish. Always posture your heart in the place of servitude. Remember, in calling you to service, the King is qualifying you for promotion; people don't qualify you. "For promotion cometh neither from the east, nor from the west, nor from the south. But God is the judge: he putteth down one, and setteth up another" (Ps. 75:6–7, KJV).

After I had served many years in the church on the local level, God promoted me to serve a church leader on a national level. During that time I was invited by a well-known pastor to enter a private conversation between him and my leader. I immediately deferred the decision to my leader, who declined the invitation he extended to me. At that point I simply left the room. I was not offended, nor did I harbor a bad attitude. I maintained my leader's trust because I obeyed her wishes and showed her respect. I passed that test.

One of my hardest-learned lessons in servanthood came by surprise. I learned that my behavior behind the scenes with my leader demanded a different protocol than when we were in public. My assumption was that I could greet my leader with a hug in public (just as I did in private). But based on my leader's demonstrated displeasure, I immediately discerned this was not a welcomed behavior in public. Of course, I was in my feelings for a moment, but I decided to use that opportunity to mature.

All leaders are not the same, and we must learn to discern how to best serve the leaders we are called to serve. With some leaders, it is OK to greet them the same way publicly as in private. Other leaders might expect you to maintain a professional manner in public and in private. Learn to read the leader's cues and follow the person's lead. The more observant and sensitive you are to your leader's expectations of you, the more you will come to realize what behavior is appropriate at any given time.

In my service to others I have learned how to serve God. My most important lesson has been how to follow the leading of the Holy Spirit. All my experiences have taught me to be sensitive to His presence, to heed His voice and to obey Him at all costs. Of course, I miss the mark sometimes, but I am still a woman after God's heart.

Relational Overflow

The Lord desires to be in relationship with us. Anyone who spends time in His presence always comes out full and overflowing, because in His presence there is fullness of joy and at His right hand there are pleasures evermore (Ps. 16:11). He wants to be your shepherd, and the Good Shepherd feeds His sheep. God feeds your needs and fills your cup. He knows the depth, width, and height of your design, because He created you and knows what your cup requires.

Only God can accurately determine what you need in your cup, so don't borrow from the cup of another. In this context, to borrow is to steal. Your portion is found only in the presence of God. If you drink from a cup that is not yours, you will forever thirst for the one that is.

When we walk closely with the Father, we soon discover that He is our overflow. Everything we need is in Him, and in Him there is no lack. He is the God of abundance and He never runs out of His essence: His goodness, grace, love, patience, forgiveness, provision, etc. Psalm 23 details what the relational, God-shepherding overflow is all about. In His care all needs are supplied. Yes, God has what you need. He provides healing, deliverance, salvation, restoration, rest, and resources, to name a few. The relational overflow we receive from being in God's presence is the fuel or power for who we are and what we do. If you are empty, it means you have run away from the Source of your supply. Never forget that you will always need God's fuel to be effective.

When it comes to operating a car, everyone knows that with the exception of the new electric vehicles, cars need fuel. Some drivers choose to travel on a full tank, many on half a tank, and others travel on fumes. But it is the driver's responsibility to put gas in his car. Typically, when drivers stop at the gas station, they fill up their own cars, right? And drivers don't borrow gas, even though they might borrow money to pay for the gas. Law-abiding citizens who drive don't siphon gas from other cars; they buy their own. What's my point? Oftentimes we look to others to meet our needs, but this can lead to severe disappointment. All able-bodied men and women are responsible for making sure they have fuel in their own tanks. God has already provided what we need, but it is our responsibility to get hitched up with the Source and get refilled. Psalm 23 (KJV) says:

> The LORD is my shepherd; I shall not want. He maketh me to lie down in green pastures: he leadeth me beside the still waters. He restoreth my soul: he leadeth me in the paths of righteousness for his name's sake. Yea, though I walk through the valley of the shadow of death, I will fear no evil: for thou art with me; thy rod and thy staff they comfort me. Thou preparest a table before me in the presence of mine enemies: thou anointest my head with oil; my cup runneth over. Surely goodness and mercy shall follow me all the days of my life: and I will dwell in the house of the LORD forever.

Psalm 23 accurately depicts how the Great Shepherd of the sheep loves and cares for His children by providing everything they need before they need it and in great abundance. Before we knew we had a need, He made provision to supply all our need "according to his riches in glory by Christ Jesus" (Phil. 4:19, KJV).

Honor Your Calling

In the grand scheme of things, this life is all about discovering how God uniquely made you to fit in His kingdom agenda. Only you will be responsible for how you steward all God entrusted to you, and only you can answer God concerning the life you chose to live here on the earth. Parents raise their children, but when those children become adults they are responsible for their own choices.

Many of us have been distracted from our life assignments by being too preoccupied with other people's lives and problems. God has not called us to be rescuers; He's called us to be stewards. If you find yourself always attending to the noise of other people's lives and problems while neglecting your own issues, this is a sign that you are off track and need to get fit. Get fit for your own life. Nothing is wrong with helping people—that's what we should do as Christians. But it should never interfere with or impede our forward progress.

Ignorance is one of Satan's most dangerous weapons, and his goal is to keep you ignorant about your identity in Christ. Satan will influence and distract you with wrong relationships, drama, and people's opinions—all to keep you off track. If you don't know who you are and what your role is in God's kingdom, the demonic realm can wreak havoc in your life. And when a Christian suffers from an identity crisis, he or she will inevitably be influenced by the spirit of witchcraft (idolatry), which seeks to control, manipulate, or hold hostage.

As a child growing up in a home bombarded with domestic violence, I assumed the role of the "rescuer." If I saw smoke, I was there. I trained myself to run to the rescue of others while losing sight of my own needs. I thought I could protect and save others and bring peace in my home, but I was not always successful.

The "rescuer child" is in constant fear of losing someone they love and losing their sense of safety and security. This child's identity is enmeshed in the well-being of others because the child thinks if others are safe then he or she can feel safe. This dysfunctional behavior paralyses the child's identity and sense of well-being and can be carried into adulthood.

Each day I am unlearning the behavior of the "rescue child" that says I'm responsible for others. Adults are responsible for their own behavior and choices. I choose to focus on where I fit and am committed to pursuing what fits me. I am tuned into my needs enough to know that if something doesn't fit, I must acquit. It has to go.

An excellent steward is one who honors his or her fit. I can truly say that I am a healthier and happier person when I focus on my own behavior and the roles I have been assigned in God's kingdom. I encourage you to be fit for the kingdom!

CHAPTER 14

Why Does It Matter?

AS I CLOSE out this book, I want to reiterate three very important themes:

- the importance of cultivating a relationship with God
- the code of conduct for the kingdom
- the need to maximize all our gifts, talents, relationships, and assignments

Cultivating an intimate relationship with the Holy Spirit is the key to learning how to properly steward our gifts, talents, and resources. He is our helper, our teacher, and our supernatural enabler. He is the anointing, Christ in us the hope of glory. The closer our walk with Him, the better we will be able to manage all that He has entrusted to us. To put it another way, proper relationship management is a prerequisite for proper resource management (stewardship).

The provisions God has stored up for His children require excellent conduct. We must learn to exercise the proper etiquette for every environment in which we have been invited. Remember, a divine invitation to stewardship is a privilege. Without the proper conduct, privileges can be revoked because misconduct is interpreted as disrespect and dishonor. Exercising the proper conduct leads to progression and great favor in the kingdom of God.

As members of the body of Christ, we must discover, cultivate, and activate the gifts and talents God has given us. When we mismanage our gifts and talents, we dishonor God, frustrate our call, and impair the function of the body of Christ. Every gift and talent that is not being used to the glory of God affects the whole body. One inactive member of the body affects the whole body. If the body is missing a toe, an arm, or an eye, the body's ability to function would be impaired. We must make good use of all the members of the body. Every member of the body of Christ needs to be activated in ministry. (See 1 Corinthians 12:12–27, NASB.)

In *Stewarding the Anointing: The Code of Conduct for the Kingdom*, I charge every member of the body of Christ with activating and maximizing their gifts and talents to the fullest. Whether you have one gift or ten, do not hide your gifts and talents but use them for God's glory.

In Matthew 25:26, Jesus called the servant with one talent "wicked and slothful" because he hid his talent (KJV). Hiding our gifts and talents is equivalent to hiding our light under a bushel. God gets no glory out of that. Jesus said, "Let your light so shine before men, that they may see your good works, and glorify your Father which is in heaven" (Matt. 5:16, KJV). We are charged with making full and proper use of the treasures that God entrusted to us so let's make Him proud.

Bibliography

Introduction

Tony Evans, "Stewardship and Ownership," Tony Evans, accessed September 21, 2019, https://tonyevans.org/stewardship-and-ownership/.

Chapter 1

Mike Murdock, *7 Wisdom Keys for Organizing Your Life* (Fort Worth, TX: The Wisdom Center, n.d), https://wisdomroombookstore.com/scripts/prodview.asp?idProduct=1072.

"10 Truths From the Book of Esther That'll Change Your Life," Redeemer Savior, accessed September 28, 2019, https://www.redeemersavior.com/book-of-esther/.

Merriam-Webster.com, s.v. "protocol," accessed September 28, 2019, https://www.merriam-webster.com/dictionary/protocol.

Beth Rifkin, "How to Develop a Protocol or Procedures," Houston Chronicle, accessed December 17, 2019, http://smallbusiness.chron.com/develop-protocol-procedures-48929.html.

Chapter 3

W. H. Westcott, "This Unction of the Holy Spirit.," STEM Publishing, accessed September 29, 2019, https://www.stempublishing.com/authors/westcott/Unction_of_the_Holy_Spirit.html.

Blue Letter Bible, s.v. "mashach," accessed September 29, 2019, https://www.blueletterbible.org/lang/lexicon/lexicon.cfm?Strongs=H4886&t=KJV.

Chapter 4

Myles Munroe, *Understanding the Purpose and Power of Women* (New Kensington, PA: Whitaker House, 2018).

Chapter 7

Blue Letter Bible, s.v. "*lypeo*," accessed November 2, 2019, https://www.blueletterbible.org/lang/Lexicon/Lexicon.cfm?trongs=G3076&t=KJV.

Chapter 8

Merriam-Webster.com, s.v. "rebellion," accessed October 29, 2019, https://www.merriam-webster.com/dictionary/rebellion.

Dr. Ron Rhodes, "How Did Lucifer Fall and Become Satan?," Christianity.com, accessed November 2, 2019, https://www.christianity.com/theology/theological-faq/how-did-lucifer-fall-and-become-satan-11557519.html.

Bibletools.org, s.v. "*halal*," accessed November 30, 2019 https://www.bibletools.org/index.cfm/fuseaction/Lexicon.show/ID/H1984/halal.htm.

Chapter 9

Dr. Rod Stodghill, in communication with the author, January 25, 2016.

Chapter 11

Merriam-Webster.com, s.v. "access," accessed November 2, 2019, https://www.merriam-webster.com/dictionary/access.

Chapter 12

Blue Letter Bible, s.v. "glory," accessed November 30, 2019, https://www.blueletterbible.org/lang/Lexicon/Lexicon.cfm?strongs=H3513&t=KJV.

Brian Taylor, "Have You Considered Finding Your Marriage Purpose?" God TV, March 22, 2019, https://godtv.com/ have-you-considered-finding-your-marriage-purpose/.

R. T. Kendall, *Total Forgiveness* (Lake Mary, FL: Charisma House, 2002, 2007), 10.

About the Author

PeriSean B. Hall exudes a passionate drive to polish people into purpose with precision. Cloaked with an uncommon grace to usher people into the very heart and presence of God, this prolific speaker, author and singer delivers words of wisdom to inspire men and women to become who they were divinely created to be.

During her professional career and ministry assignments, PeriSean has illumined the following platforms: seminar/workshop facilitator, news reporter/producer, TV/radio show and LIVE events producer, radio personality, worship leader, and emcee and stage performer. She is also the author of *My Mama Told Me: Motherly Wisdom for Everyday Living*, her debut book, released in 2014. In 2019, PeriSean was approved and confirmed as a Commissioned Minister by the ministry leaders in her home church, Oak Cliff Bible Fellowship in Dallas, TX where Dr. Tony Evans is senior pastor.

Author's Resource Page

Contact:
445 East FM 1382, Suite #3-158
Cedar Hill, TX 75104
Website: www.perisean.com

Social Media Links
https://www.instagram.com/perisean/
https://www.linkedin.com/in/periseanhall/
https://www.facebook.com/perisean
https://www.facebook.com/authorperiseanbhall/

Book: My Mama Told Me

CD: This Is Where I Belong

Books and Music CD are available via:

www.perisean.com

Amazon:
https://www.amazon.com/s?k=my+mama+told+me+perisean&ref=nb_sb_noss

KDP: http://a.co/ioejBbh

PeriSean's CD is also available on iTunes

Ministry Donations via:
Zelle: PeriSean Hall at periseanenterprises@gmail.com
PayPal: paypal.me/PeriSeanEnterprises

Magazine Feature Link:
http://voyagedallas.com/interview/meet-perisean-hall-perisean-enterprises-sole-proprietor-dallas/

www.ingramcontent.com/pod-product-compliance
Lightning Source LLC
Chambersburg PA
CBHW071406290426
44108CB00014B/1700